Louise
Nov. 1983

D1476022

Celebration Cookbook

100 YEARS OF DEDICATION TO THE KID IN ALL OF US.

1883   1983

Bologna Song

My bo-log-na has a first name, it's O-S-C-A-R. My bo-log-na has a sec-ond name, it's M-A-Y-E-R. Oh! I love to eat it eve-ry day and if you ask me why I'll say... ..... 'cause Os-car May-er has a way with B-O-L-O-G-N-A.

Table of Contents

ISBN 0-8249-3018-5
Copyright © MCMLXXXIII by Oscar Mayer & Co.
All rights reserved.
Printed and bound in the United States of America
Published by Ideals Publishing Corporation

®The Name Oscar Mayer and the Oscar Mayer Logo are
Trademarks of Oscar Mayer & Co., Inc.

A Frank Look at the History of Sausage

How did Caesar gain advantage over the Barbarians? Skilled fighting? Perhaps. But more likely with his cuisine. Was Caesar a master chef? Well, no. But while enemy soldiers lost precious hours hunting, butchering and cooking, Caesar and company simply dined on preserved meats in casings ... and won.

You see, the first convenience food was not the burger to go. It was ... sausage! And as early as 900 B.C., the ancients were chopping meat, seasoning it with spices and herbs, curing it with salts and sugars before smoking, cooking or drying it into hams, bacon and sausage.

Adventurers arriving at distant shores discovered a whole world of spices and herbs, and they cleverly added these distinctive new flavorings to their sausage recipes. European villages developed their own specialties. Bologna actually originates from Bologna, Italy. From

Frankfurt, Germany came the frankfurter, and from Vienna, Austria ... the wienerwurst (Wien is actually the German spelling of Vienna).

Settlers coming to America brought along their old world

recipes. However, with certain spices unavailable they had to use their ingenuity. But from such inventiveness came the delicious all-American favorites. And to that burst of creativity all we can say is ... hot dog!

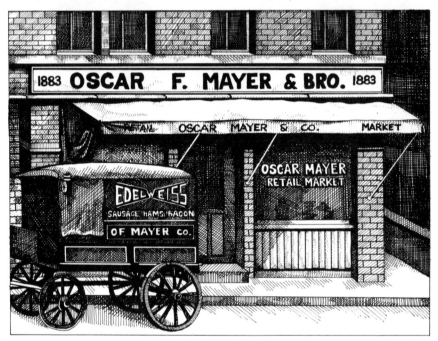

One Man's Link from the Old World to the New

Nearly a decade after the Civil War, the wheels were turning on a newly finished train that spanned the continent, and the Industrial Age was blossoming into a productive and progressive era. It was a time when Americans could hope to build a dream.

It was for this New World that a strong-willed Bavarian boy of 14 set out, leaving his family and home. Starting as a "butcher's boy" in Detroit, young Oscar F. Mayer worked his way up to an apprenticeship in the busy Chicago stockyards. He wrote home, requesting his brother Gottfried to study sausage-

making from the old Bavarian masters. And finally, on September 1, 1883, young Oscar opened his own market with his brother. They made and sold Old World Sausage and Westphalian ham. Their motto was "quality first" and it paid off.

When their lease was up after five years, Oscar, Gottfried and a third brother, Max (who came over to do the accounting), bought their own building. That site is still the present location of the Oscar Mayer plant in Chicago. They kept selling. Soon, a horse-drawn wagon carrying "Edelweiss" products made deliveries. There were

several employees by now, all adhering to the quality standards set by the Mayer brothers. In fact, Oscar Mayer was one of the first American meat producers to join the newly created federal inspection program in 1906.

By the time the founder's son, Oscar G. Mayer, graduated from college, the company was ready to expand further. In 1919 they bought a meat packing plant from a farmers cooperative in Madison, Wisconsin. It's now the headquarters of a multi-billion dollar meat business whose motto is still "quality first."

Word Gets Around

Many people young and old still remember "Little Oscar" and his "Wienermobile," but few recall the glass-paneled Oscar Mayer delivery wagon pulled by a sleek coach horse named "Strawberry".

Until 1904, Strawberry and the fancy wagon helped draw attention to Oscar Mayer products. But the real advertising came by word of mouth.

In 1929, the company took a major step in a new direction. Sausage employees began putting a paper band with the company name on it around every fourth wiener. The Oscar Mayer wieners stood out from competitors' products in the retailer's case. That success led to increased efforts to brand identify additional products.

The introduction of "Little Oscar" in 1936 marked another first. From the start, the midget chef and his sausage-shaped vehicle, the Wienermobile, caught the public fancy. He appeared in parades giving out "wiener whistles," conducted cooking demonstrations and toured the country visiting with shoppers at supermarket openings.

And then came television. In 1963, the "Wiener Jingle" captured the imagination of young and old everywhere. Kids of all ages have been singing "Oh, I wish I were an Oscar Mayer wiener" ever since. And Andy, the little boy on the cover whose "bologna has a first name," still makes us smile.

Wiener Jingle

Coney Island Hot Dogs

10 servings

- ½ pound ground beef
- 1 medium onion, chopped
- 1 can (8 oz.) tomato sauce
- 1 teaspoon chili powder
- ½ teaspoon Worcestershire sauce
- 1 package (16 oz.) Oscar Mayer wieners
- 10 hot dog buns

Cook beef and onion in skillet on medium heat, stirring often until beef is browned. Add tomato sauce, seasonings and wieners. Bring to a boil; turn down heat. Simmer 10 minutes. Serve wieners in buns; top with sauce.

Best Ever Potato Salad

5 servings

- 10 slices Oscar Mayer bacon
- ¾ cup mayonnaise
- 1 tablespoon prepared mustard
- 2 teaspoons sugar
- 1 teaspoon salt
- 4 cups cooked and diced potatoes
- 4 hard-cooked eggs, chopped
- 1 stalk celery, chopped
- 1 small onion, chopped
- ½ medium green pepper, chopped

Cut bacon into 1-inch pieces. Cook in skillet on medium-low heat until crisp. Drain bacon, reserving 2 tablespoons drippings in skillet. Remove skillet from heat. Add mayonnaise, mustard, sugar and salt; mix well. Combine potatoes, eggs, celery, onion and green pepper in bowl. Add dressing and toss. Stir in bacon. Cover. Chill several hours before serving.

Country Sausage and Apples

4 servings

- 1 package (12 oz.) Oscar Mayer "Little Friers" pork sausage links
- 2 large cooking apples, cored and cut into eighths
- ½ cup cream
- ½ cup brown sugar
- ½ teaspoon cinnamon
  Hot pancakes or waffles

Cook links according to package directions; pour off drippings. Add apples to skillet. Cover. Cook on medium 5 minutes until apples are tender-crisp. Combine cream, brown sugar and cinnamon to make sauce. Top pancakes with links, apples and sauce.

Hot Bacon Spinach Salad

6 serving

- 1 package (16 oz.) Oscar Mayer bacon
- 1 egg, beaten
- ½ cup water
- ⅓ cup sugar
- ¼ cup vinegar
- ⅛ teaspoon pepper
- 12 ounces fresh spinach, torn into bite-size pieces

Cut bacon into 1-inch pieces. Cook in skillet on medium-low until crisp. Drain, reserving ¼ cup drippings in skillet. With whisk, stir in remaining ingredients, except spinach. Simmer 10 minutes. Pour over spinach. Toss and serve immediately.

Throw an Ice Cream Social and Bring Back the '90s

The telephone had just been invented, and there was plenty to talk about. Burlesque, Vaudeville and Minstrel shows entertained ... Wild Bill Hickok put on a rootin' tootin' traveling show, and the slim-waisted Gibson Girl was the standard of beauty. Electricity was just starting to light up the parlors, and iced tea, ice cream cones and hot dogs in buns were novelties.

America's favorite get-together was the ice cream social on the lawn. You can throw an 1890s party to remember, with some of these summer recipes and plenty of iced tea. Corsettes and parasols were all the rage for women. Men wore high starched collars. Knickers and hoops were the fashion for kids.

Ask your guests to come in costume, hire a photographer, and send each guest home with an old-fashioned photo souvenir.

Bicycling was big—and bicycles had one big wheel up front and a tiny back one. If you can rent two, set up an obstacle course for bike races. How about a croquet match? Or have a make-your-own Sundae bar.

Your invitations can be reproductions of turn-of-the-century ads for elixirs, corsettes and fancy baby carriages. Find some old telephone boxes, wash tubs and rug beaters. (Remember, this was before women's rights!) Go Victorian—decorate with lace doilies and set up the Victrola. Serve old-fashioned favorites like Coney Island Hot Dogs, Best Ever Potato Salad and homemade ice cream. Have a great time!

Coney Island Hot Dogs, Be Ever Potato Salad

Bring the Glitzy Twenties Back with a Roar

Oh, those fabulous twenties. The roaring (crowds cheer as Babe Ruth hits his 60th home run), soaring (Lindberg flies the "Spirit of St. Louis"), never boring (Al Capone celebrates St. Valentine's Day . . . HIS way). It was a time of jazz, flappers' razzmatazz . . . and the crazy antics of Charlie Chaplin, Buster Keaton and the Keystone Kops.

To capture it all again, you can throw a roaring "Prohibition Party" of your own. Send out invitations with the "secret" password into your Speak Easy (Tell 'em Roxy sent ya). Invite the gangsters, the classy Great Gatsby's, the flappers and the college rah-rah's with sweater vests and caps. Hire a dance instructor, find some old Big Band, Rudy Vallee and Louis Armstrong records, and you'll have your guests doing the Charleston and Varsity Drag in no time! Stage a "raid," with some of your friends dressed as Keystone Kops.

Decorations could include giant feathers, a mirrored ball hanging from the ceiling (today we'd call it a disco ball) . . . posters of those romantic silent movie stars, and lots of glitz. You can set up an old bathtub with ice, and use open violin cases (a la Capone) to serve chips and crackers or bread. All drinks, according to Speak Easy frequenters, were served in innocent-looking coffee mugs.

Scalloped Potatoes and Ham

4 servings

4 medium potatoes, peeled and sliced ¼-inch thick
3 cups (about 1 lb.) cubed Oscar Mayer ham
1 small onion, chopped
¼ cup flour
½ teaspoon salt
⅛ teaspoon pepper
¼ cup butter
1½ cups milk

Cover bottom of 10x6-inch lightly greased glass baking dish with single layer potatoes, ham and onion. Sprinkle with part of the flour, salt and pepper. Dot with some butter. Repeat layers until ingredients are used, reserving 2 tablespoons butter. Pour milk over top; dot with remaining butter. Bake in 350°F oven 1 hour until potatoes are tender and top is golden brown.

Smokie Spanish Rice

4 servings

1 package (12 oz.) Oscar Mayer "Smokie Links"*
1 cup uncooked long grain rice
1 can (16 oz.) stewed tomatoes
1 can (8 oz.) tomato sauce
½ cup water
1 bay leaf
½ teaspoon ground thyme

Cut Smokie Links into 1-inch pieces. Combine in large skillet with remaining ingredients. Bring to a boil. Cover. Turn down heat. Simmer 30 minutes, stirring occasionally.

*Or use 1 package (12 oz.) Oscar Mayer "Little Friers" pork sausage links, cooked according to package directions.

Flaky Pie Crust

2 pie crust

⅔ cup Oscar Mayer lard
2 cups sifted flour
1 teaspoon salt
5 to 6 tablespoons cold water

Measure lard and chill if desired (for a flakier crust). Mix flour and salt together in a bowl. Cut in lard with pastry blender or 2 knives until particles are the size of peas. Sprinkle 5 tablespoons water evenly over flour mixture. Toss lightly with fork just to moisten; overmixing will toughen pastry. Dough should feel moist but not sticky. If more water is needed, sprinkle additional tablespoon of water over loose flour in bottom of bowl. Shape into 2 balls.

Single crust pies: Roll out 1 ball of pastry on floured surface to a circle 2 inches larger than inverted pie pan. Carefully fit into pie pan and flute edge. If filling is to be added to baked crust, pierce unbaked crust generously with a fork. Bake in 450°F oven 10 to 12 minutes or until lightly browned.

Double crust pie: Roll out 1 ball pastry on floured surface, following directions for 1 crust pie. Roll out other ball of pastry and cut slits for steam to escape. Place over filling. Flute edge. Bake as filling recipe directs.

Tips:
1. *Use pastry cloth which has been lightly floured (easy handling and clean-up).*
2. *Flatten ball to ½-inch with hands before rolling (less cracked edges).*
3. *Use light strokes, working from center out when rolling (evens crust).*
4. *Fold pastry over rolling pin and place over pie pan (facilitates handling dough and reduces tearing).*
5. *Ease pastry into pie pan taking care not to stretch (reduces shrinkage).*

Old Fashioned Baked Beans

12 servings

1 package (1 lb.) dry navy beans
6 cups cold water
1 teaspoon salt
10 slices Oscar Mayer bacon
½ cup brown sugar
¼ cup molasses
1 medium onion, chopped
2 teaspoons dry mustard

Rinse beans. Combine beans and water in large saucepan or Dutch oven. Cover; bring to a boil. Boil 2 minutes. Remove from heat; let stand 1 hour or overnight. Add salt. Simmer partially covered 1 hour or until beans are tender. Drain, reserving liquid. Cut bacon into 1-inch pieces. Combine uncooked bacon, brown sugar, molasses, onion and dry mustard with beans in Dutch oven or 2-quart bean pot. Add 1¾ cups reserved liquid. Bake uncovered in 300°F oven 5 hours. Add additional water if necessary.

For Slow Cooker: (2½ to 5 quart). Prepare recipe as above using only ¾ cup reserved liquid; stir. Cover and cook on low for 10 hours (no stirring necessary), or on high for 4 hours, stirring occasionally.

Wieners 'n Sauerkraut

4 servings

1 package (16 oz.) Oscar Mayer wieners
1 medium onion, chopped
1 tablespoon vegetable oil
1 jar (32 oz.) sauerkraut, drained
1 tablespoon brown sugar

Combine wieners, onion and oil in skillet. Heat on medium 10 minutes, stirring occasionally. Stir in sauerkraut and brown sugar. Cover. Heat 5 minutes more.

Fried Bologna and Eggs

1 serving

2 slices Oscar Mayer bologna
1 teaspoon butter
2 eggs, beaten

Cut meat into quarters. Melt butter in skillet on medium heat. Add meat. Heat 2 to 3 minutes until lightly browned. Add eggs. Continue to cook and stir until eggs are set but still moist. Serve with catsup, if desired.

Jubilee Ham with Rum Te Dum Sauce

12 servings

1 can (3 lb.) Oscar Mayer ham
1 can (8¼ oz.) crushed pineapple, with liquid
½ cup orange juice
½ cup brown sugar
¼ cup raisins
1 tablespoon cornstarch
1 teaspoon dry mustard
¼ teaspoon ground ginger
⅛ teaspoon ground cloves
⅛ teaspoon ground nutmeg
2 tablespoons rum

Heat ham according to package directions. Combine remaining ingredients except rum in saucepan. Bring to a boil. Turn down heat. Simmer 5 minutes until thickened, stirring occasionally. Stir in rum. Brush on ham last 30 minutes of heating. Serve remainder as sauce.
200 calories/serving

Super Subs

4 servings

1 package (12 oz.) Oscar Mayer "Variety-Pak" cold cuts
4 submarine buns (6 to 7-inch)
 Italian dressing
 Leaf lettuce
8 slices process American cheese
2 tomatoes, thinly sliced
1 small onion, sliced and separated into rings

Arrange 1 slice of each meat flavor in buns which have been sprinkled with Italian dressing. Add lettuce, cheese, tomato and onion.

Celebrate the Fourth of July in Grand Ol' Style

*C*elebrate Independence Day in the "Spirit of '76." With a plume pen, have your guests sign in on a scroll resembling the Declaration of Independence. Play rousing patriotic music or even hire a "fife and drum" corps. Fill your

backyard with red, white and blue balloons and streamers.

Read famous quotes ("Give me liberty or give me death") and have everyone guess the colonists who said them. The kids might enjoy "Minutemen" relay races. Or pass out crayons so they can design their own version of Betsy Ross' stars and stripes. Play a few games of the all-American sport—baseball. But this time, make it the rebels versus the redcoats.

Little Friers Coffeecake

6 servings

1 package (12 oz.) Oscar Mayer "Little Friers" pork sausage links
1 package (19 oz.) apple-cinnamon coffeecake mix
1 egg
½ cup milk

ook pork sausage according to ackage directions. Arrange cooked ausage spoke-fashion in bottom of -inch round cake pan. Top ausage with apple slices and pping mix packet. Prepare batter ccording to package directions sing egg and milk; pour over ausage, apples and topping. Bake 400°F oven 25 minutes or until oothpick inserted in center comes ut clean. Loosen from sides of an; invert onto serving platter.

Swiss Ham Baked Fondue

6 servings

½ pounds Oscar Mayer ham, cut into ½-inch cubes
½ pound natural Swiss cheese, cut into ½-inch cubes
4 slices dry bread, torn into pieces
½ cup dry white wine
2 tablespoons kirsch, optional
3 tablespoons butter
3 tablespoons flour
1 cup milk
3 eggs, beaten

ombine ham, cheese and bread in quart casserole. Blend wine and rsch; pour over mixture, stirring moisten. Melt butter in ucepan. Stir in flour. Add milk wly; heat to boiling, stirring nstantly. Remove from heat. Stir eggs 1 at a time. Pour over ixture. Bake in 350°F oven 1 ur.

Bacon Egg Puff Pie

6 servings

1 package (16 oz.) Oscar Mayer bacon
1 can (8 oz.) refrigerated crescent roll dough
1 tomato, thinly sliced
1 cup (4 oz.) shredded Cheddar cheese
2 eggs, separated
½ cup (4 oz.) sour cream
¼ cup flour
2 green onions, finely chopped
Dash pepper

Cut bacon into 1-inch pieces. Cook in skillet on medium-low until crisp; drain. Separate dough into 8 triangles. Place in ungreased 9-inch pie pan, pressing edges together to form crust. Layer on crust: bacon, tomato and cheese. Beat egg whites until stiff; set aside. Combine egg yolks, sour cream, flour, onion and pepper in large mixing bowl; mix well. Fold in egg whites. Pour over cheese layer. Bake in 350°F oven 40 minutes or until toothpick inserted in center comes out clean.

Eggs Benedict

3 servings

6 eggs
1 package (6 oz.) Oscar Mayer Canadian bacon
3 English muffins, split, toasted, buttered
Easy Hollandaise Sauce*

Lightly grease a 10-inch skillet. Add 1½-inches water (about 6 cups). Bring to a boil. Turn down heat. Break 1 egg onto a saucer; gently slide into water. Repeat with remaining eggs. Simmer 3 to 5 minutes just until set, basting often with water. Remove with slotted spoon. Meanwhile, place Canadian bacon in unheated skillet. Heat on medium 5 minutes, turning once. Top each muffin half with Canadian bacon slice, egg and Hollandaise sauce.

Easy Hollandaise Sauce:
½ cup sour cream
½ cup mayonnaise
1 teaspoon prepared mustard
2 teaspoons lemon juice

Combine ingredients in saucepan. Heat on medium-low about 5 minutes, stirring frequently.

There's No Other Like a Mother

Mother's Day is the second Sunday in May. It's a time to thank Mom for all she's done for you. (Even though she does make you do your homework and wash behind your ears.) Whistler did it in a painting . . . Al Jolsen did it in a song, on one knee. And you can do it with a luxurious breakfast in bed served with a single flower and a card you made yourself. And the best gift of all? Clean up afterwards!

Arty Party

The rule has always been—no drawing on the walls, right? Make an exception and cover the walls with a long, seamless sheet of butcher paper, shelf paper or wrapping paper. If you use messy paints (tempera or water colors) you can make instant smocks out of plastic garbage bags. Just cut a hole in the bottom for the head and an armhole on either side. Give the artists a theme (space, sports, nature, animals, etc.) or just let them create. Have everybody sign their work of art. It's a lasting souvenir of the gathering—and a great idea for a going away party or a special anniversary.

Breakfast Cookies

32 cookies

- 1 can (3 oz.) Oscar Mayer bacon bits*
- ½ cup butter, softened
- 1 egg
- 2 tablespoons frozen orange juice concentrate
- ¼ cup sugar
- 1 cup flour
- 1 teaspoon baking powder
- 2 cups corn flakes
- ¼ cup wheat germ

Combine first 5 ingredients in large bowl; blend well. Stir in remaining ingredients. Shape into 1-inch balls. Place 2 inches apart on ungreased cookie sheet. Flatten with fork dipped in flour. Bake in 350°F oven 12 to 15 minutes until golden brown. Wrap and store in refrigerator.

*Or use 10 slices Oscar Mayer bacon, cooked and crumbled.

Breakfast Sandwich

6 sandwiches

- 5 Oscar Mayer wieners
- ½ cup (2 oz.) shredded process American cheese
- ½ cup chopped ripe olives
- ¼ cup mayonnaise
- 12 slices bread
- 3 eggs, beaten
- ⅓ cup milk
- ⅛ teaspoon salt

Cut wieners into penny slices. Combine with cheese, olives and mayonnaise in bowl. Spread on 6 slices bread. Top each with another bread slice. Combine eggs, milk and salt in pie pan. Dip both sides of each sandwich quickly into egg mixture. Place on hot greased griddle or greased skillet. Cook until browned on both sides, turning once.

Note: Sandwiches can be made day before, cooled, wrapped individually in foil and refrigerated. Next day, heat in 350°F oven 15 minutes.

Doughnut-Wrapped Little Smokies

16 doughnuts

- 1 package (5 oz.) Oscar Mayer "Little Smokies"
- 1 package (8 oz.) refrigerated biscuits
  Cinnamon-sugar or Powdered sugar
  Jelly or jam
  Oil for frying

Cut each biscuit in half; press dough flat. Wrap dough around each Little Smokie, pinching seams to seal. Interesting shapes can be formed by tying and twisting dough around sausages. Deep fat fry about 1 minute until golden brown. Drain on paper towels. Roll in cinnamon-sugar or sprinkle with powdered sugar. Serve with jam.

Quiche Lorraine

6 serving

- 1 package (16 oz.) Oscar Mayer bacon
- 1 (9-inch) frozen deep-dish pie crust, thawed
- 1 cup (4 oz.) shredded Swiss cheese
- 1 tablespoon finely chopped onion
- 4 eggs, beaten
- 2 cups half-and-half
- ⅛ teaspoon pepper
  Dash nutmeg
  Paprika

Cut bacon into ½-inch pieces. Cook in skillet on medium-low until crisp; drain. Sprinkle bottom of pie crust with bacon, cheese and onion. Combine eggs, half-and-half, pepper and nutmeg. Pour over bacon and cheese. Sprinkle with paprika. Bake in 425°F oven 15 minutes; reduce heat to 325°F. Bake 40 minutes more or until knife inserted in center comes out clean. Let stand 10 minutes before serving.

Microwave: Cut bacon into ½-inch pieces; place in shallow glass baking dish. Cover with paper towel. Microwave at HIGH 14 to 16 minutes to desired crispness stirring twice with 2 forks to separate pieces. Drain. Transfer pie crust to 9-inch glass pie plate. Microwave at HIGH 4 minutes until dry and opaque, rotating plate after two minutes. Sprinkle bottom of crust with bacon, cheese and onion. Set aside. Combine eggs, half-and-half, pepper and nutmeg in 1-quart glass casserole. Microwave at HIGH 4½ to 5 minutes, stirring after three minutes. Stir mixture; pour over bacon and cheese. Sprinkle with paprika. Cover with waxed paper. Microwave at HIGH 3 minutes, rotating plate after one and one-half minutes. A knife inserted in center should come out clean when quiche is done. Let stand 5 minutes before serving.

Frittata

2 servings

4 slices Oscar Mayer New England brand sausage
1 tablespoon butter
3 eggs, beaten
3 tablespoons milk
2 tablespoons grated Parmesan cheese
2 tablespoons chopped fresh vegetables, as desired (onion, green pepper, tomato, mushrooms, broccoli, zucchini, olives)

Cut meat in half. Arrange around edge of small skillet. Meat slices should extend above egg mixture when added, but not beyond rim of pan. Melt butter in skillet. Combine remaining ingredients and pour into skillet. Cover. Cook on low 10 minutes or until set.
170 calories/serving

Microwave: Place meat pieces in 1-quart round glass casserole. Microwave at HIGH 1 minute. Combine egg mixture as above. Pour over meat. Cover. Microwave at HIGH 2 to 2½ minutes, stirring after one minute.

Bacon Beer Brunch Bread

1 loaf

1 package (16 oz.) Oscar Mayer bacon
3 cups self-rising flour
3 tablespoons sugar
1 can (12 oz.) beer

Cut bacon into ½-inch pieces. Cook in large skillet on medium-low until crisp; drain. Combine bacon, flour and sugar in large bowl; stir to coat bacon. Add beer; stir just to moisten. Pour into greased 9-inch round baking pan or 9x5-inch loaf pan. Bake in 375°F oven 45 to 50 minutes until lightly browned.

Wagon Master Corn Bread

6 servings

8 slices Oscar Mayer "Lean 'n Tasty" breakfast strips
1 package (8½ oz.) corn muffin mix
1 can (8¾ oz.) whole kernel corn, with liquid
1 egg
Pancake syrup

Overlap breakfast strips, spoke-fashion, in bottom of heavy 10-inch skillet. Beat egg in medium bowl. Blend in muffin mix and corn. Pour over breakfast strips. Cover. Cook on low heat 20 minutes or until toothpick inserted in center comes out clean. Loosen corn bread from edge and invert on plate. (If strips stick to pan, lift off with spatula and replace in design on corn bread.) Serve with syrup.

Microwave: Arrange breakfast strips, spoke-fashion, in 8-inch round glass baking dish. Beat egg in medium bowl. Blend in muffin mix and corn. Pour over breakfast strips. Cover with waxed paper. Microwave at HIGH 5 to 5½ minutes, rotating dish after three minutes. Corn bread is done when toothpick inserted in center comes out clean. To serve, loosen corn bread from edge and invert on plate. Serve with syrup.

Bacon Strata

6 servings

1 package (16 oz.) Oscar Mayer bacon
1 medium onion, finely chopped
8 oz. fresh mushrooms, sliced
6 slices bread
1 cup (4 oz.) shredded Cheddar cheese
4 eggs
2 cups milk
1 teaspoon prepared mustard

Cook bacon in large skillet on medium-low heat until crisp. Drain, reserving drippings. Roll 6 slices while still warm to make bacon curls; set aside. Grease bottom of 13x9-inch baking dish with 1 tablespoon reserved bacon drippings. Add onion and mushrooms to 3 tablespoons of remaining bacon drippings. Cook on medium heat until tender. Arrange bread on bottom of dish. Top with mushroom-onion mixture, cheese and bacon. Beat eggs in medium bowl. Blend in milk and mustard. Pour over bacon. Bake in 350°F oven 35 minutes or until puffed and golden brown. Garnish with bacon curls.

Note: May be prepared several hours to a day ahead. Cover and refrigerate. Bake as directed above.

Hansel and Gretel Party

Your guests won't need to follow bread crumbs to find your house if you bake gingerbread. Invite them over to build a storybook gingerbread house. Collect pictures of other gingerbread houses for some creative inspiration. Buy lots of trimming goodies beforehand—gumdrops for doorknobs, licorice sticks for door frames and trim, and vanilla icing for rooftop snow. When the masterpiece is complete, take your own snapshots. For a happy ending, donate your storybook dream, along with a few fairy tale books, to a local children's hospital or orphanage.

Appealing Appetizers

Ribbon Cubes

16 appetizers

1 package (8 oz.) Oscar Mayer chopped ham*
2 slices square pumpernickel bread
1 package (3 oz.) cream cheese and chives, softened

Spread all meat and bread slices with cream cheese. Stack meat and bread in following order: 3 slices ham, 1 slice bread, 2 slices ham, 1 slice bread, 3 slices ham. Wrap tightly in plastic wrap. Chill. Cut into 16 cubes to serve.

*Or other Oscar Mayer square sliced meat (honey loaf, luncheon meat, smoked cooked ham).

Pinwheels

32 appetizers

1 package (8 oz.) Oscar Mayer luncheon meat
1 package (3 oz.) cream cheese, softened
   Round crackers or party rye bread

Spread meat slices with cream cheese. Roll first slice; join meat edges to start second slice and continue to roll 4 slices into log. Repeat using remaining 4 slices. Wrap and chill thoroughly. Cut into ¼-inch slices. Serve on rye bread or crackers.

Zesty Bacon Dip

1 cup

10 slices Oscar Mayer bacon
1 cup (8 oz.) sour cream
1 tablespoon horseradish
1 teaspoon Worcestershire sauce

Cut bacon into ½-inch pieces. Cook in skillet on medium-low until crisp; drain. Combine remaining ingredients. Chill. Add bacon pieces just before serving.

Ribbon Cubes, Pinwheels, Little Wieners Wellington, Rumaki, Tidbits, Wedges, Bells

Little Wieners Wellington

16 appetizers

1 package (4 oz.) Oscar Mayer braunschweiger liver sausage
1 (9-inch) frozen pie shell
1 package (5½ oz.) Oscar Mayer "Little Wieners"

Soften braunschweiger at room temperature for 30 minutes or place in bowl and mash with fork. Thaw pie shell for 10 minutes. Remove from pan and flatten dough. Repair tears and cracks. Spread braunschweiger on dough. Cut into 5 strips. Divide the 2 end strips in half; cut the 3 center strips into fourths. Roll each piece of dough around a Little Wiener, pinching seam to seal. Place seam-side down on baking sheet. Bake in 375°F oven 20 to 25 minutes until lightly browned.

To Make Ahead: Prepare as above but do not bake. Cover and refrigerate several hours or overnight. Bake in 375°F oven 30 minutes or until lightly browned.

Rumaki

40 appetizers

1 package (16 oz.) Oscar Mayer bacon
1 can (8 oz.) whole water chestnuts
1 pound chicken livers
1 bottle (10 oz.) teriyaki sauce
   Toothpicks

Cut bacon slices in half. Slice water chestnuts into 2 or 3 pieces. Cut chicken livers into bite-size pieces. Wrap bacon around water chestnuts and chicken livers. Secure with toothpicks. Marinate in teriyaki sauce at least 1 hour. Bake in 400°F oven 20 to 25 minutes.

Or prepare as above using:
   shrimp
   crabmeat
   oysters
   pineapple
   olives
   mushrooms

Trivia and Treats

Tired of watching TV game shows while your wealth of knowledge remains behind the scenes? Pass the word—you're staging a quiz show at home! Have your guests "come on down" after you've pored through trivia and reference books for questions. Set up a variety of categories and difficulty levels. Tape segments of famous films on a video recorder and ask contestants to name the movie and its star performer. Give everyone a bell to ring when they can "name that tune." Authentic game shows require official judges as well as an emcee. And remember, you'll be in "jeopardy" without prizes to award. If the price isn't right for a pair of round trip tickets, you can "bet your life" that the winner will love a "Trivia Champ" t-shirt. Create one easily with iron-on letters. Have plenty of Tidbits and ABC Appetizers around for munching during the station breaks. After the show, sandwiches like "Dog Gones" may help console those who didn't hit the jackpot!

Aphrodite's Appetizers

72 appetizers

2 packages (8 oz. each) Oscar Mayer braunschweiger liver sausage
1 package (8 oz.) cream cheese, softened
1 tablespoon dried chives
1 package (1 lb.) phyllo dough, thawed
1 cup (½ lb.) butter, melted

Blend braunschweiger, cream cheese and chives in mixer or food processor. Unroll dough; cover with lightly moistened towel to prevent drying and cracking. Place 1 sheet of dough on work surface. Brush dough with melted butter. Top with another sheet of dough; brush with butter. Repeat, stacking dough 4 sheets high. If dough becomes torn or ragged, brush with butter. Cut stack into 6 lengthwise strips; cut each strip in half crosswise. Place 1 teaspoon braunschweiger filling at end of each strip. Fold dough flag-fashion around filling to form triangle; pinch edges and brush with butter to seal. Repeat until all sheets of dough are used. Place meat triangles on shallow baking pan. Bake in 400°F oven 15 minutes until golden brown. Serve warm. Freeze extras. To reheat, place frozen triangles on cookie sheet and heat in 400°F oven 15 minutes.

Tidbits

32 appetizers

1 package (6 oz.) Oscar Mayer smoked cooked ham
4 ounces Swiss cheese, cut into 32 cubes
2 tablespoons butter
1 tablespoon lemon juice
Dash garlic powder

Cut each meat slice into 4 strips. Wrap each around a cheese cube fastening with a toothpick. Melt butter in skillet or chafing dish; stir in lemon juice and garlic powder. Place tidbits in skillet; heat 5 minutes just until cheese softens, turning occasionally. Serve with sauces.

Caper Cream Sauce:
Combine ½ cup mayonnaise, ¼ cup capers
Chili Dip: Combine ½ cup sour cream, 1 tablespoon chili sauce, 1 tablespoon horseradish, ½ teaspoon onion powder, ¼ teaspoon paprika
Dill Mayonnaise: Combine ½ cup mayonnaise, 2 teaspoons dill weed, ½ teaspoon onion powder, ⅛ teaspoon bottled hot pepper sauce

Microwave: Assemble tidbits as above. Melt butter in shallow glass baking dish at HIGH about 30 seconds; stir in lemon juice and garlic powder. Place tidbits in circular pattern around edge of dish. Microwave at HIGH 1 minute until cheese softens.

Cotto Cheese Crisp

4 appetizer

2 slices Oscar Mayer cotto salami
1 large flour tortilla, 7-inch diameter
¼ cup shredded Monterey Jack cheese
2 tablespoons chopped green chilies
3 ripe olives, sliced
1 tablespoon butter

Cut meat slices in quarters. Top tortilla with 2 tablespoons cheese meat, chilies, remaining cheese ar olives. Melt butter in skillet on medium. Add tortilla to skillet. Cover; heat 5 minutes or until cheese melts. Cut into wedges to serve.

Microwave: Arrange as above o plate. Omit butter. Microwave at HIGH 1 minute until cheese melt rotating after thirty seconds.

Snappy Snacks

30 appetize

5 slices Oscar Mayer New England brand sausage
1 cup (4 oz.) shredded Farmer's cheese
1 green onion, finely chopped
1 tablespoon mayonnaise
30 rye crackers

Cut stacked meat slices into 6 wedges; separate. Combine chees onion and mayonnaise. Top each cracker with 1 meat piece and 1 teaspoon cheese mixture. Broil 4 inches from heat until cheese bubbles.

Microwave: Place 6 snacks in circle on a paper plate. Microwa at HIGH 30 seconds, rotating pl after fifteen seconds. Repeat wit remaining appetizers.

Flavored Bacon Treats

40 appetizers

1 package (16 oz.) Oscar Mayer bacon
Coating

Parmesan bacon: ⅔ cup grated Parmesan cheese

Onion bacon: ½ cup cornmeal + 1 tablespoon onion powder

Cinnamon-sugar bacon: ½ cup sugar + 2 teaspoons cinnamon

Seasoned bacon: 1 envelope coating mix for pork

Orange bacon: ¾ cup sugar + grated peel of orange

Nutty bacon: 1 cup finely ground pecans

Italian bacon: ½ cup seasoned Italian bread crumbs

Cut bacon slices in half. Place coating mix in shallow dish. Dip bacon in coating. Arrange on rack in shallow pan. Bake in 400°F oven 10 to 15 minutes until crisp.

Bacon Stuffed Mushrooms

18 appetizers

1 pound fresh mushrooms (about 2-inch diameter)
2 tablespoons chopped onion
2 tablespoons butter
1 slice bread, torn into small pieces
1 cup (4 oz.) shredded Cheddar cheese
1 can (3 oz.) Oscar Mayer bacon bits

Wipe mushrooms well with damp cloth. Remove stems from mushrooms; set aside caps. Chop stems. Cook onions and chopped mushroom stems in butter until tender; add bread pieces. Remove from heat; stir in cheese and bacon bits. Press filling into caps. Place in shallow baking pan. Bake in 400°F oven 15 minutes until cheese is melted. Serve warm.

Microwave: Combine onions, mushroom stems and butter in small glass mixing bowl. Microwave at HIGH 5 minutes or until tender, stirring once after two minutes. Stir in remaining ingredients. Fill mushroom caps. Arrange 6 caps in circle on paper plate. Microwave at HIGH 1½ minutes.

Zurich Dip

2 cups

1 package (8 oz.) cream cheese
1 cup (8 oz.) sour cream
1 teaspoon instant minced onion
⅛ teaspoon garlic powder
1 can (3 oz.) Oscar Mayer bacon bits
Paprika
Fresh vegetables for dipping

Combine cream cheese, sour cream, onion and garlic; blend well. Stir in bacon bits, reserving some for garnish. Spoon into shallow 1-quart glass casserole. Bake in 350°F oven 20 minutes. Sprinkle with paprika and reserved bacon bits. Serve warm with fresh vegetables and crackers.

Braunschweiger Party Log

20 servings

1 package (8 oz.) Oscar Mayer braunschweiger liver sausage
1 package (3 oz.) cream cheese, softened
1 can (3 oz.) Oscar Mayer bacon bits*
Crackers or party rye bread

Remove braunschweiger from package, taking care to retain meat in its log shape. Frost log with cream cheese and roll in bacon bits. Chill. Place on small lettuce-lined tray with crackers, party rye or French bread.

*Or use 10 slices Oscar Mayer bacon, cooked and crumbled.

Marseilles Tarts

36 appetizers

10 slices Oscar Mayer bacon
1 can (8 oz.) refrigerated butterflake dinner rolls
2 eggs
½ cup sour cream
1 medium tomato, finely chopped
¼ cup finely chopped onion
½ teaspoon basil leaves

Cut bacon into ½-inch pieces. Cook in large skillet on low until crisp; drain. Separate dough into 12 pieces. Divide each piece into 3 sections. Press dough sections into 1¾-inch diameter muffin (tart) cups, stretching dough slightly to form shell. Combine remaining ingredients and bacon pieces in bowl. Divide mixture evenly among shells, using a rounded teaspoon for each. Bake in 375°F oven 15 minutes or until golden brown. Serve warm.

Microwave: Place 10 frozen tarts in circle on paper plate. Microwave at HIGH 2½ to 3 minutes rotating plate after two minutes.

Cocktail Sausages

64 appetizers

4 packages (5 oz. each) Oscar Mayer "Little Smokies" or "Little Wieners"*
Sauce
Toothpicks

Prepare 1 of the sauces below in a chafing dish or saucepan. Add "Little Smokies" or "Little Wieners" and heat about 5 minutes longer, stirring occasionally. Serve with toothpicks.

Barbecue: Heat 1 bottle (18 oz.) barbecue sauce

Cheese Fondue: Heat together 1 can (11 oz.) Cheddar cheese soup and ¼ cup dry white wine

Currant: Heat 2 jars (10 oz. each) currant jelly

Little Rubies: Heat together 1 can (21 oz.) cherry pie filling and ¼ cup Rosé wine

Orange Nutmeg: Combine ½ cup sugar, 2 tablespoons cornstarch and ½ teaspoon nutmeg. Stir in 1½ cups orange juice. Cook on medium heat stirring constantly until mixture boils and thickens. Stir in 1 can (11 oz.) mandarin orange segments, drained.

Microwave: Place 1 package "Little Smokies" or "Little Wieners" in 1-quart glass casserole. Add ¼ cup sauce. Cover with plastic wrap. Microwave at HIGH 3 minutes. (Makes 16).

*Or use 1 package (16 oz.) Oscar Mayer wieners cut into 1-inch pieces.

I Hate Monday Party

Celebrate it on Tuesday. You'll be too depressed on Monday.

Tropical Ham Salad

4 servings

1 package (8 oz.) Oscar Mayer ham slice or ham steaks
1 can (16 oz.) grapefruit sections
1 avocado
1 can (11 oz.) mandarin orange segments, drained
¼ cup coconut
4 lettuce cups

Dressing:
½ cup (4 oz.) sour cream
1½ teaspoons sugar
½ teaspoon horseradish
¼ teaspoon salt
   Dash dry mustard

Cut ham into ½-inch pieces. Drain grapefruit sections, reserving liquid. Peel avocado; cut into chunks. Dip avocado into grapefruit liquid to prevent discoloration. Combine ham, grapefruit, avocado, oranges and coconut. Spoon into lettuce cups. Blend dressing ingredients with 1 tablespoon grapefruit liquid. Serve with salad.
325 calories/serving

Salade au Poivre

4 servings

1 package (6 oz.) Oscar Mayer smoked cooked ham
2 medium red-skin potatoes, cooked
   Watercress
1 can (16 oz.) sliced beets, drained
1 hard-cooked egg

Dressing:
1 cup (8 oz.) plain yogurt
¼ teaspoon lemon pepper

Combine dressing ingredients and refrigerate at least 1 hour to allow flavors to blend. Cut ham slices in half. Cut potatoes into 8 wedges. Wrap each potato wedge with half slice ham. For each salad: place meat-wrapped wedges on plate lined with watercress. Arrange beets between wrapped wedges. (Salad plates can be wrapped in plastic wrap and refrigerated until serving.) Just before serving, press egg yolk through sieve or strainer. Sprinkle on salad. Chop egg white. Stir into dressing. Spoon over salad.
185 calories/serving

Salad Oscar

4 serving

1 package (12 oz.) Oscar Mayer "Cheese Smokies"
1 head lettuce, torn into bite-siz pieces
½ medium green pepper, sliced into rings
2 onion slices, separated into rings
1 medium tomato, cut into wedges
¼ cup sliced fresh mushrooms
¾ cup creamy French dressing
½ cup salad croutons

Cut Smokies into ½-inch slices. Arrange lettuce and vegetables or plates. Combine Smokies and French dressing in saucepan. Hea to boiling, stirring often. Reduce heat to low. Cover. Heat 5 minutes. Top salad with Smokie mixture and croutons. Serve immediately.

Curried Fresh Fruit Boats

4 servin

1 package (8 oz.) Oscar Mayer honey loaf
2 pineapples
1 banana
1 pear
12 strawberries
½ cup blueberries

Dressing:
1 carton (8 oz.) pineapple yogur
¼ teaspoon curry powder

Cut meat into 1-inch strips; roll and set aside. Cut each pineapple in half lengthwise; remove inside leaving shells intact. Core and di pineapple. Slice banana, pear and strawberries. Toss with pineapple and blueberries. Fill each pineapple half with fruit mixture Top with meat rolls. Blend dressing ingredients. Serve over salads.
305 calories/serving

You'll be the Star at an Academy Awards Night Party!

A *blockbuster party on Academy Awards night guarantees rave reviews. Have your invitations resemble movie posters: A "premiere" event is "coming soon"—produced and directed by (you!). Along with your invitation, mail ballots listing nominations for each of the five major categories. Your guests will have time to pick their winners, and the ballot can serve as an "admission" ticket. Print each guest's name on a star made from foil-covered cardboard. Attach the* stars to the back of director's chairs.

Serve "Salad Oscar" and "Specialty of the House" sandwiches before turning on the TV. After the show, determine which ballot was most accurate. Announce the winner dramatically—"the envelope please"—"and the winner is . . ." Award a prize for "Best Performance on a Ballot" (a package of Oscar Mayer wieners—what else!) Then prepare yourself for yet another acceptance speech!

Run for the Roses

If you can't get to Kentucky this May, bring the Blue-grass State to your home—host a Kentucky Derby party! Turn your party area into the Churchill Downs clubhouse by setting up a makeshift ticket booth. Use play money or poker chips at your win, place and show windows. Copy all information on the horses—their odds, weight and jockey—from the sports section of your newspaper. Hand your friends an official program as they come through "the gate."

Have plenty of mint juleps for your "grandstand" guests while they're waiting for the day's ninth race. But place your bets on a juicy, whole barbecued ham, and your party's sure to end with a "photo finish."

Alsatian Salad

4 servings

1 package (12 oz.) Oscar Mayer "Variety-Pak" cold cuts
5 pickled mild yellow peppers
1 green pepper
2 medium onions, thinly sliced
3 kosher dill pickles, coarsely chopped
3 hard-cooked eggs, cut into wedges

Dressing:
¼ cup mayonnaise
3 tablespoons sour half 'n half
2 teaspoons dill weed
⅛ teaspoon oregano leaves
   Dash pepper

Cut meat, yellow and green peppers into ¼-inch strips; toss with onion and pickles. Blend together dressing ingredients. Pour over salad. Garnish with egg.

New England Sausage Salad

6 servings

2 packages (8 oz. each) Oscar Mayer New England brand sausage
7 ounces shell macaroni, cooked
½ cup (2 oz.) shredded Cheddar cheese
½ cup sliced celery
¼ cup chopped green pepper
¼ cup chopped sweet pickle

Dressing:
½ cup mayonnaise
½ cup sour cream
1 teaspoon lemon juice
½ teaspoon onion powder

Cut meat into ¼-inch strips. Combine with remaining salad ingredients in large bowl. Blend together dressing ingredients. Pour over salad. Toss. Cover. Chill 1 hour.

Salad Primavera

2 servings

1 package (8 oz.) Oscar Mayer ham slice or ham steaks*
1 package (10 oz.) frozen Italian-style vegetables in sauce
2 tablespoons red wine vinegar with garlic
1 tablespoon vegetable oil
2 ounces fettucini or spaghetti, cooked
1 head Boston lettuce
1 tablespoon grated Parmesan cheese

Cut ham into 1-inch cubes. Bring vegetables, vinegar and oil just to a boil in large skillet. Add cooked noodles and ham. Cover. Chill several hours. Arrange on lettuce-lined platter. Sprinkle with cheese.

*Or use 1 package (6 oz.) Oscar Mayer smoked cooked ham

Gourmet Picnic Salad

8 servin[g]

1 package (8 oz.) Oscar Mayer honey loaf
1 package (6¾ oz.) long grain and wild rice mix, cooked
2 stalks celery, coarsely chopp[ed]
2 green onions, finely chopped
1 cup (4 oz.) shredded Swiss cheese
1 can (14 oz.) artichoke hearts, drained and cut in half

Dressing:
¼ cup lemon juice
¼ cup vegetable oil
2 teaspoons Dijon mustard
¼ teaspoon pepper

Cut meat into 1-inch cubes. Combine with cooked rice, celery, onion and cheese. Combine dressing ingredients. Pour over meat mixture; mix well. Garnish with artichokes. Cover. Chill several hours.

Greek Salad

4 servin[gs]

1 package (8 oz.) Oscar Mayer olive loaf
1 medium head lettuce
1 cucumber, pared, cut into chunks
1 small onion, thinly sliced
10 cherry tomatoes
½ cup calamata (Greek-style) [or] ripe olives
4 ounces feta cheese, cubed

Dressing:
½ cup olive oil
½ cup lemon juice
¼ teaspoon pepper

Cut meat into 1-inch cubes. Tea[r] lettuce into small pieces. Place i[n] salad bowl. Add olive loaf, cucumber and onion. Combine dressing ingredients. Pour over salad. Toss. Garnish with tomatoes, olives and cheese.

Fruit & Ham Flan

8 servings

1 package (8 oz.) Oscar Mayer chopped ham
1 package (17 oz.) date bread mix
1 cup water
1 egg
1 package (8 oz.) cream cheese, softened
Assorted fresh fruit: sliced bananas, sliced kiwi, strawberries, pineapple chunks, blueberries

ut meat into quarters. enerously grease and flour a 12 14-inch pizza pan. Combine ead mix, water and egg in bowl. read evenly in pan. Bake in 5°F oven 15 minutes until nter springs back when touched htly. Do not overbake. Cool. read with cream cheese; arrange eat and fruit in circular pattern top. Cut into wedges to serve.

Secretary's Day Switch

*T*he third week in April is set aside to officially thank secretaries. So . . . start by switching places . . . for an hour or a day. The boss gets the coffee, types and files. At lunchtime, put on an awards banquet. Each boss can bring in a dish for a bountiful buffet. Entertain with live music (call your groups The Typos or The Rubber Band). Then present awards. It'll be a great day and a great way to tell your secretary she's "just your type."

BLT Salad

4 servings

10 slices Oscar Mayer bacon
1 medium head lettuce, torn into bite-size pieces
2 medium tomatoes, sliced
1 cup salad croutons

Dressing:
½ cup mayonnaise
2 tablespoons milk
1 teaspoon prepared mustard
½ teaspoon sugar

Cut bacon slices in half. Cook in large skillet on medium-low until crisp; drain. Arrange lettuce, tomatoes, croutons and bacon on salad plates. Combine dressing ingredients. Spoon over salad just before serving.

Wiener Sauerkraut Salad

6 servings

1 package (16 oz.) Oscar Mayer wieners
2 cups sauerkraut, drained
1 cup thinly sliced radishes
¼ cup chopped green pepper
½ cup sour cream
½ cup mayonnaise
Lettuce leaves

Cut wieners into ½-inch pieces. Combine with sauerkraut, radishes and green pepper. Cover. Chill 1 hour. Blend sour cream and mayonnaise together for dressing. Toss with sauerkraut just before serving. Serve on lettuce leaves.

Wisconsin Salad

4 servings

1 package (8 oz.) Oscar Mayer ham slice
1 package (10 oz.) frozen peas, thawed
1 cup chopped celery
1 cup (4 oz.) Cheddar cheese, cut into cubes
⅓ cup mayonnaise
2 teaspoons prepared mustard
Lettuce leaves

Cut ham into ½-inch cubes. Combine with remaining ingredients, except lettuce. Cover. Chill 1 hour. Serve on lettuce leaves.

Other salad favorites

- **Seven Layer Salad:** Layer lettuce, celery, onion, green peppers, peas, mayonnaise with sugar, crumbled bacon and shredded cheese in a bowl.

- **Chef's Salad:** Pile high julienne strips of ham, salami and cheese on a bed of mixed salad greens.

- **Wilted Lettuce Salad:** Tear leaf lettuce into bite-size pieces and top with the hot bacon dressing from the Hot Bacon Spinach Salad recipe.

- **Bacony Cole Slaw:** Add cooked, crumbled bacon to your favorite cole slaw.

- **Hodgepodge Salad:** Combine leftover vegetables (peas, beans or cauliflower) with strips of cold cuts (bologna, summer sausage or luncheon meat), and marinate in favorite bottled salad dressing.

- **Ham Waldorf Salad:** Add ½-inch cubes of ham to Waldorf salad for a main dish meal. Use plain yogurt with cinnamon as a low-cal dressing.

- **Smokie Taco Salad:** Toss Smokie Links cut into thin slices with salad greens, corn chips, onions, cheese, kidney beans and Green Goddess salad dressing.

Hearty Hot Hero

4 servings

- 1 loaf (1 lb.) French bread
- ¼ cup butter
- 1½ teaspoons Italian herb seasoning
- 1 cup alfalfa sprouts
- 1 tomato, thinly sliced
- 1 small onion, sliced and separated into rings
- 1 package (8 oz.) Oscar Mayer cotto salami
- 1 package (6 oz.) Oscar Mayer smoked cooked ham
- 10 mild pickled pepperocini
- 4 slices process American cheese, cut diagonally

Slice bread lengthwise. Spread both halves with butter; sprinkle with Italian seasoning. On bottom half, layer sprouts, tomato, onion, folded meats, peppers and cheese. Add top of bread. Wrap in foil. Bake in 350°F oven 45 minutes. Cut into 4 portions.

To Make Ahead: Prepare as above. Wrap and refrigerate. Increase baking time 10 minutes.

Microwave: Prepare as above setting aside cheese and top. Cut into 4 portions. Place 2 bottom portions on paper plates. Microwave at HIGH 2½ minutes; add cheese and top half of bread. Rotate plates. Microwave 1½ minutes more or until cheese melts. Repeat with remaining 2 portions.

BLT Club

1 sandwich

- 3 slices Oscar Mayer bacon
- 3 slices bread, toasted Mayonnaise
- 2 slices tomato
- 3 slices turkey breast Leaf lettuce

Cook bacon in skillet on medium-low until crisp; drain. Spread bread with mayonnaise. Assemble sandwich as follows: bread, lettuce, tomato, bacon, bread, lettuce, turkey, bread.

Ham Cordon Bleu

8 servings

- 1 package (6 oz.) Oscar Mayer smoked cooked ham
- 2 tablespoons horseradish sauce
- 8 slices turkey breast
- 8 slices natural Swiss cheese, each 4 - inches square
- ¼ cup butter, melted
- ½ cup seasoned crumbs
- 8 small French rolls Toothpicks

Spread each slice of meat with horseradish sauce; top with turkey and cheese. Roll and secure with toothpicks. Brush with butter and roll in seasoned crumbs. Place on baking sheet. Bake in 350°F oven 10 minutes or until cheese just begins to melt. Remove toothpicks; serve in rolls.

Microwave: Assemble as above in 12x7-inch glass baking dish. Cover with plastic wrap. Microwave at HIGH 3½ to 4 minutes until cheese just begins to melt.

Note: Cut into thirds for appetizers.

Specialty of the House

1 sandwich

- 2 slices Oscar Mayer bacon
- 1 large slice rye bread, toasted
- 1 leaf lettuce
- 2 slices Oscar Mayer braunschweiger
- 2 slices tomato
- 4 slices avocado
- 2 tablespoons Thousand Island dressing

Cook bacon according to package directions; drain. Place toasted bread on dinner plate. Top with lettuce leaf and braunschweiger. Arrange tomato and avocado over braunschweiger. Top with bacon. Spoon dressing over top.

Waffle Grilled Sandwich

1 sandwic

- 2 slices Oscar Mayer bologna
- 1 slice process American cheese
- 2 slices bread Butter Jam or jelly

Place 2 slices meat and 1 slice of cheese between bread. Spread outside of sandwich with butter. Grill sandwich in heated waffle iron until bread is golden brown and cheese is melted. Top with jam or jelly.

Note: Sandwiches may also be grilled in skillet or burger grill.

A Lunchtime Surprise

If you pack a lunch for your loved ones, surprise them with their favorite cold cut sandwich . . . cut in the shape of a heart. Fill a holiday brown bag with sandwiches cut into Christmas trees and bells. Shamrock sandwiches are great for St. Pat's Day, and pumpkins and ghosts make perfect spooky Halloween treats.

Ham Apple Yodeler

1 serving

3 slices Oscar Mayer smoked cooked ham
1 raisin English muffin, split and toasted
4 teaspoons plain yogurt
  Lettuce
2 fresh apples slices
  Cinnamon

Roll up each meat slice; cut in half. Spread muffin halves with half of yogurt; sprinkle with cinnamon. Top each with lettuce, apple slice and 3 meat roll-ups. Add dollop of yogurt; sprinkle with cinnamon.
275 calories/serving

Zorba's Pocket Sandwich

8 sandwiches

1 package (8 oz.) Oscar Mayer cotto salami
1 package (8 oz.) Oscar Mayer New England brand sausage
4 pita breads (6 to 7 inch diameter), cut in half
8 lettuce leaves

Salad Mixture:
1 medium cucumber, thinly sliced
1 medium onion, thinly sliced
12 pitted ripe olives, sliced
¾ cup low-cal Italian dressing

Combine and chill salad mixture; marinate at least 1 hour. To assemble each sandwich, place 2 meat slices and 1 lettuce leaf in "pocket" of pita bread. Fill pockets with salad mixture.

195 calories/serving

Monte Cristo

4 servings

1 package (6 oz.) Oscar Mayer smoked cooked ham
4 slices Swiss cheese, each 4 inches square
4 slices turkey breast
8 slices bread
  Oil for frying
  Confectioner's sugar
  Raspberry jam
  Toothpicks

Batter:
1½ cups flour
2 teaspoons baking powder
¼ teaspoon salt
2 eggs
1½ cups milk

Layer 2 slices ham, 1 slice cheese and 1 slice turkey on each of 4 slices of bread. Top with remaining bread slice. Press sandwich firmly together; cut into quarters. Secure with toothpicks. Heat oil to 375°F in heavy 3-quart saucepan or deep fat fryer. To prepare batter: combine flour, baking powder and salt in medium bowl. Beat eggs and milk; stir into flour mixture until smooth. Dip each sandwich in batter to coat well. Fry 3 minutes or until golden brown on both sides. Drain on paper towels. Remove toothpicks; sprinkle with sugar. Serve with jam.

Ham Croissant Sandwich

4 sandwiches

1 package (3 oz.) cream cheese, softened
½ teaspoon dill weed
4 croissants, split horizontally
4 lettuce leaves
1 package (6 oz.) Oscar Mayer smoked cooked ham
8 tomato slices
12 cucumber slices

Combine cream cheese and dill weed; spread on bottom half of each roll. Top each with lettuce leaf, 2 meat slices, 2 tomato slices, 3 cucumber slices and top half of roll.

240 calories/serving

Lunch Abroad

2 sandwiches

1 package (3 oz.) cream cheese, softened
¼ teaspoon curry powder
4 slices whole wheat bread
2 lettuce leaves
1 package (6 oz.) Oscar Mayer smoked cooked ham
¼ cup chutney

Combine cream cheese and curry. Spread on bread. Arrange lettuce and meat on 2 slices. Spread chutney on remaining slices. Close sandwiches. Cut each in half to serve.

Other Sandwich Favorites

Sandwich spread: Using the knife blade, process ham, bologna or wieners in food processor until meat is a fine texture. Combine with pickle relish and mayonnaise.

Grilled cheese 'n bacon: Add fully cooked bacon slices to cheese sandwich. Butter outside of sandwich and grill in skillet until browned on both sides.

Bacon cheeseburger: Top a cheeseburger with 2 slices of cooked bacon for a real feast.

Denver sandwich: Add cubes of cooked ham to eggs scrambled with onion, green pepper and mushrooms.

Peanut butter and bacon: Crumble cooked bacon and sprinkle over toast spread with crunchy-style peanut butter.

Antipasto Sandwich

4 servings

- 1 loaf (1 lb.) unsliced bread, about 10-inches long
- 1 head lettuce
- 1 package (8 oz.) Oscar Mayer hard salami
- 8 ounces provolone cheese, thinly sliced
- 24 ripe olives
- 2 tomatoes, cut into wedges
  Pickled mild Italian peppers
  Italian salad dressing

Slice bread lengthwise into 4 flat pieces. Top each slice with lettuce, meat, cheese, olives, tomatoes and peppers. Serve with Italian salad dressing.

Muffaletta

6 sandwiches

- 1 package (8 oz.) Oscar Mayer hard salami
- 6 slices (1 oz. each) provolone cheese
- 6 hard rolls

Salad Mixture:

- 1 bottle (8 oz.) Italian dressing
- 2 stuffed green olives, sliced
- 2 ripe olives, sliced
- 1 small zucchini, sliced
- 1 small onion, sliced and separated into rings

Combine ingredients for salad in small bowl; marinate 1 hour. To assemble each sandwich, place 4 slices meat, 1 slice cheese and ⅓ cup salad mixture in roll.

Epicurean Delight

4 servings

- 2 packages (8 oz. each) Oscar Mayer honey loaf
- 8 slices rye bread
- 1 package (10 oz.) French-style green beans, thawed
- ½ cup process cheese spread
- 1 package (5 oz.) frozen French fried onion rings

Fold 4 meat slices diagonally. Arrange on 2 slices of bread. Place on oven proof plate or baking sheet. Top with ¼ of green beans and cheese spread. Garnish with onion rings. Repeat. Bake in 350°F oven 20 minutes.
260 calories/serving

Smokie Link Reuben

4 sandwiches

- 1 package (12 oz.) Oscar Mayer "Smokie Links"
- 8 slices pumpernickel or dark rye bread
- 1 cup (8 oz.) sauerkraut, well drained
- ¼ cup Thousand Island dressing
- 4 slices process Swiss cheese, each about 4 inches square
- ¼ cup butter

Cut Smokie Links in half lengthwise. Place 4 halves on bread slice. Top with ¼ cup sauerkraut, 1 tablespoon dressing, 1 cheese slice and another bread slice. Repeat. Butter outsides of sandwiches. Place in heavy skillet. Cover. Heat on medium-low 10 minutes. Turn; heat uncovered 10 minutes more or until cheese melts.

Microwave: Toast 4 slices bread. Place 1 slice on each plate. Cut Smokie Links in half lengthwise. Arrange 4 halves cut side up on toast. Top with ¼ cup sauerkraut, 1 tablespoon dressing and 1 cheese slice. Microwave each sandwich at HIGH 1½ to 2 minutes. Serve open face.

Shift into a Nifty Fifties Sock Hop

*I*f you remember the fifties, you probably think of those crazy poodle skirts . . . hoola hoops . . . bobby socks . . . and 45s (the top ten by Buddy Holly, Fats Domino, Sha Na Na). Ponytails and scarves around the neck for girls, combed-back hair and D.A.'s for the guys. Rockin' round the clock. James Dean. Marilyn Monroe. "Leave It to Beaver" and "I Love Lucy" were some of the favorite TV shows. Television, in fact, was something new!

You can bring it all back to life again with a good ol' dance-the-night-away sock hop. Roll up the carpets, put out the food and spin those records. Or rent a juke box. Hire a disc jockey, or ask for volunteers from the guests. For the younger set . . . or the young at heart, have a hoola-hoop contest.

If you want to go outdoors, hayrides were a favorite in the fifties. Start off with a moonlight ride, and have hot cider, cocoa and submarine sandwiches waiting at home. THEN put on the records, kick off your shoes and jitterbug the night away!

Hot Dogs 'n Brown Bags

Cheese Hounds

4 sandwiches

4 slices Oscar Mayer bacon
4 Oscar Mayer wieners
2 slices process American cheese, each cut into 4 strips
4 hot dog buns
   Toothpicks

Cut a lengthwise 4-inch pocket in each wiener; stuff each with 2 strips cheese. Wrap each stuffed wiener tightly with 1 bacon slice; secure with toothpicks. Place on broiler pan, cut side down. Broil inches from heat 6 minutes. Turn over; broil 4 minutes more or until cheese melts and bacon is crisp. Remove toothpicks. Serve in buns.

Microwave: Place 4 bacon slices between layers of paper towel on paper plate. Microwave at HIGH 2 to 2½ minutes until bacon is lightly crisp. Cut a lengthwise 4-inch pocket in each wiener; stuff each with 2 strips of cheese. Wrap each stuffed wiener tightly with 1 bacon slice; secure with toothpicks. Arrange around outside edge of plate. Microwave at HIGH until cheese melts: 2 wrapped wieners—minute; 4 wrapped wieners 1¾ to 2 minutes. Remove toothpicks. Serve in buns.

Dilly of a Ham Sandwich

1 sandwich

2 slices Oscar Mayer smoked cooked ham
1 Kaiser roll
1 teaspoon butter
1 slice process American cheese
1 tablespoon mayonnaise
⅛ teaspoon dill weed
¼ cup alfalfa sprouts

Place meat on bottom half of buttered roll; top with cheese slice. Spread mayonnaise on top of cheese; sprinkle with dill weed. Top with sprouts and top half of roll.

Corn Dogs

10 servings

1 package (16 oz.) Oscar Mayer wieners
10 wooden skewers
   Oil for deep frying

Batter:
½ cup flour
⅓ cup cornmeal
1 tablespoon sugar
1½ teaspoons dry mustard
¾ teaspoon baking powder
½ teaspoon salt
1 tablespoon shortening
½ cup milk
1 egg

Insert skewers lengthwise into wieners. Combine dry batter ingredients in bowl. Cut in shortening. Add milk and egg; blend until smooth. Pat wieners dry with paper towel to allow batter to adhere. Dip each wiener into batter, using spoon to coat wiener evenly. Allow excess batter to drip into bowl. Heat oil in heavy skillet or deep fat fryer to 375°F. Arrange coated wieners 3 at a time in hot oil, turning with tongs after 10 seconds to set batter. Cook 2 minutes longer or until golden brown, turning several times. Serve hot.

Crunchy Cucumber and Salami

4 sandwiches

1 package (8 oz.) Oscar Mayer salami
4 round hard rolls, cut
1 cup low-fat cottage cheese
2 teaspoons horseradish
1 cucumber, thinly sliced
4 thin green pepper rings

Place 4 slices meat on bottom half of each roll. Combine cottage cheese and horseradish in bowl; spoon over meat. Top with cucumber slices and green pepper ring. Add top half of roll.
310 calories/sandwich

Note: This sandwich may be made a day ahead and refrigerated.

Blanket Smokies

6 servings

1 package (12 oz.) refrigerated ready-to-bake apple turnovers
6 Oscar Mayer "Smokie Links"

Assemble turnovers placing Smokie Link inside turnover with filling. Bake according to package directions until golden brown. Let stand 5 minutes before serving.

At a Puppet-Making Party, The Fun Speaks for Itself

Here's a kids' party idea that takes the cake. Make puppets, and wrap up with a show for the parents. Make them from old socks and glue on felt ears, button eyes and yarn hair. Or try cereal box puppets using little single serving boxes and construction paper faces. Everybody can work on one storybook theme (The Three Little Pigs . . . Little Red Riding Hood . . . Peter Pan) or make up their own characters. They can even make puppets that are portraits of themselves!

Crunchy Cucumber and Salami, Cheese Hound

Hot Dogs... Hooray!

There must be over a hundred ways to celebrate with hot dogs. Here are just a few favorite ideas:

- **Barbecued Hot Dogs:** Brush with barbecue sauce and grill outside.

- **Bowser Buns:** Slash wieners in ½-inch intervals cutting almost but not quite through. They curl when heated. Serve on round buns with mustard and relish.

- **Calcutta Canine:** Spread mayonnaise mixed with a touch of curry on a toasted bun, then top a wiener with raisins, coconut, chutney and chopped peanuts.

- **Chinese Chews:** Stir-fry wiener strips with oriental vegetables and serve over chow mein noodles.

- **Crunchy Cats:** Dip wieners in mustard, then roll in seasoned coating mix and bake until golden and heated through.

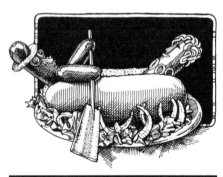

Dog Paddle

Rowboat: Hot dog bun   **Frank's Arms:** Little wieners   **The Franks:** Two Oscar Mayer wieners or beef franks   **Eyes:** Pimento and olive slices or onion rings   **Noses:** Cheese   **Mustache:** Parsley   **Necklace:** Onion rings   **Hair:** Canned cheese spread   **Waves:** Onion rings   **Tophat:** Carrot slice and pickle attached with pretzel stick   **Oar:** Soda straw with carrot slice

Attach eyes, noses, mustache, mouth and necklace with cheese spread.

- **Double Cheese Dogs:** Combine bleu cheese and cream cheese; spread on buns.

- **Greek Goddess:** Marinate olives, cucumber, tomato and onions with thin slices of beef franks, then slip into a pita pocket for a classic delight.

- **Hawaiian Hot Dogs:** Heat wieners in sweet 'n sour sauce with chunks of pineapple, green pepper and tomato. Serve on toasted buns.

- **Hobo Hot Dogs:** Franks 'n beans together in a bun ... heat'em both over the campfire and enjoy life on the road.

Hot Rod Dog

Car Body: Oscar Mayer wiener or beef frank in a bun   **Windshield:** Onion slice   **Smile:** Ripe olive slice   **Hood:** Cheese slice decorated with catsup and mustard   **Headlights:** Olives attached with pretzel sticks   **Wheels:** Red onion slices and pickle and hubcaps put together with pretzel sticks   **Steering Wheel:** Pretzel ring   **Goggles:** Onion rings   **Driver:** Little wiener with cherry tomato head attached with pretzel stick

Attach windshield and goggles with cheese spread.

- **Kraut Dogs:** Heat sauerkraut with caraway and a touch of sugar. Pile on top of a hearty beef frank.

- **Pizza Pups:** Top English muffins with pizza sauce, thin slices of wieners and shredded mozzarella cheese. Broil just 'til cheese melts.

Long John Frankie

Body: Oscar Mayer wiener or beef frank cut in half   **Arms:** Little Wieners   **Coat:** Wiener wrap   **Buttons:** Pimentos   **Feet:** Radish slices   **Eye & Patch:** Black olive   **Beard:** Parsley   **Hat:** Green pepper   **Pipe:** Pimento olive and pretzel stick   **Sail:** Bread with crust removed on a soda straw mast   **Raft:** Toasted bread with canned cheese spread

Attach hat, buttons, eye, eye patch, and beard with cheese spread.

- **Russian Wolfhounds:** Heat wieners in Russian dressing, the serve on rye ... Russian, of course.

- **Tahitian Treats:** Combine pineapple, orange, bananas and coconut with sour cream, then mound on a wiener in a toasted bun.

- **Taco Dogs:** Heat wieners in tomato sauce flavored with taco seasonings; serve in shells with taco toppings.

Dog Gones

8 sandwiches

2   medium carrots, shredded
¼   cup raisins
¼   cup chopped peanuts
¼   cup chopped celery
¼   cup low-cal mayonnaise
1   package (8 oz.) Oscar Mayer honey loaf
8   hot dog buns

Combine carrots, raisins, peanuts, celery and mayonnaise in bowl. Place about 2 tablespoons of mixture on each slice of meat. Roll and place in buns.

Pigs In A Blanket

8 servings

1 package (16 oz.) Oscar Mayer
  Jumbo beef franks
8 strips Cheddar cheese,
  4x½x¼-inch each
1 can (8 oz.) refrigerated
  crescent roll dough

ut lengthwise pocket in each
ank to within ½ inch of ends;
sert cheese strips. Separate
ough into 8 triangles. Place
vorite condiment and frank on
ortest side of each triangle; roll
p. Place on ungreased baking
eet, cheese side up. Bake in
75°F oven 12 to 15 minutes until
lden brown.

icrowave: Wrap each Pig in a
lanket in a paper towel. Place on
per plate. Microwave each at
IGH 35 to 45 seconds rotating
ate halfway through heating.

Wiener Hoagie

10 sandwiches

1 package (16 oz.) Oscar Mayer
  wieners
0 hard rolls
  Mayonnaise
2 tomatoes, sliced into 5 slices
  each
0 slices provolone cheese
  (about 8 oz.)
1 red onion, sliced
0 lettuce leaves
1 jar (4 oz.) sliced pimiento

eat wieners according to package
rections. Spread rolls with
ayonnaise. Cut wieners
ngthwise, almost through, and
read open. Place wieners in rolls.
op with tomato, cheese, onion,
ttuce and pimiento.

Brown Bag Specials

*Carrying lunch need not be boring
or time consuming. Try making
sandwiches ahead and freezing—
they'll thaw before lunch—or plan
to reheat a favorite in the
microwave. Try breadless
combinations or inside out
versions.*

• Spread each slice of bread to the
  edges with softened butter (this
  keeps the bread from getting
  soggy).

• Wrap each sandwich separately;
  label and freeze (cold cuts,
  peanut butter and cheese all
  freeze well). Sandwiches thaw in
  three hours.

• Wrap lettuce, cole slaw, tomato
  and hard-cooked eggs separately
  (they don't freeze). Ditto for
  mayonnaise, jelly and salad
  dressings.

• Use different kinds of bread—
  raisin, English muffins, croissants,
  bagels, bread sticks or pita—
  keeps lunch from getting boring.

• Heat soup and pour in thermos.
  Add wieners. Come lunchtime,
  have hot wieners with soup on
  the side.

• Tuck coleslaw inside a meat slice
  for a quick breadless sandwich.

• Cutting calories? Try 90% fat-
  free cold cuts—50 calories or less
  per slice.

• Spread meat slices with cheese or
  mustard, then wrap around a
  bread stick or giant pretzel.

• Grill sandwiches at home; reheat
  in microwave—just wrap in a
  paper napkin to keep the bread
  from getting soggy.

Three-Ring Circus

Turn your basement or
backyard into a Big Top
*with colorful streamers, helium
balloons, circus posters and
animal decorations. Try to find
distorted mirrors to make
funny faces in. In the first ring,
you have games. Choose
according to kids' interests and
age. Toss peanuts into bucket
. . . throw nerf balls to knock
boxes over. Form a human
calliope by assigning each child
a note.*

*Then bring in the clowns! Hire
a local funster to entertain
everyone with stunts and tricks.
Some have trained pets, some
know magic. But all clowns
have a way of making everyone
laugh.*

*Third ring features gift-
opening. And as for food,
decorate your cake with animal
crackers. Serve ice cream
clowns by decorating a scoop of
ice cream with a clown's face in
jelly beans, then topping with
an upside down cone. Store in
freezer till ready. Invitations?
Write on a balloon with felt tip
pens and send, uninflated, in
an envelope (include your
phone number on a separate
piece of paper, just in case
your invitation pops).*

Double Cheese Ham Skillet

4 servings

- 1 package (6 oz.) Oscar Mayer smoked cooked ham
- 1 package (3 oz.) cream cheese, softened
- 3 green onions
- 2 tablespoons butter
- 1 package (11 oz.) frozen French-style rice
- 1 cup frozen peas
- ¾ cup (3 oz.) shredded Cheddar cheese

Spread ham slices with cream cheese. Top each with green onion; roll up. Combine butter and ⅓ cup water in large skillet. Add rice, seasoning from packet and peas. Bring to a boil, stirring to break apart. Place ham rolls on rice. Cover. Heat on medium-low 5 to 7 minutes. Sprinkle with cheese. Cover. Heat 2 minutes more.

Swiss Hamlets

2 servings

- 1 package (8 oz.) Oscar Mayer chopped ham
- 4 slices Swiss cheese, 4 inches square
- 1 package (10 oz.) frozen broccoli spears, thawed
  Toothpicks
- 1 package (1 oz.) white sauce mix
- ¼ cup sour cream
- 1 tablespoon prepared mustard
- ½ teaspoon dill weed

Top 2 slices of meat with slice of cheese and ¼ of broccoli; roll and secure with toothpicks. Place in small shallow baking dish. Repeat. Prepare white sauce mix according to package directions. Stir in remaining ingredients. Top meat with sauce. Bake in 350°F oven about 30 minutes. Remove toothpicks before serving.

Care Package Casserole

8 servings

- 1 package (16 oz.) Oscar Mayer bacon
- 1 package (8 oz.) medium noodles
- 1 cup (8 oz.) cottage cheese
- 1 package (8 oz.) cream cheese
- ½ cup (4 oz.) sour cream
- 5 green onions, chopped
- 2 cans (8 oz. each) tomato sauce
- 1 package (16 oz.) Oscar Mayer wieners
- 1 tablespoon chopped fresh parsley

Cut bacon into 1-inch pieces. Cook in skillet on medium-low until crisp; drain. Cook noodles according to package directions. Combine bacon with noodles. Place half of bacon-noodle mixture in a 13x9-inch baking dish. Combine cottage cheese, cream cheese, sour cream and green onions in a bowl. Spread cheese mixture over noodles. Top with remaining bacon-noodle mixture. Arrange wieners on top. Pour tomato sauce over all and sprinkle with chopped parsley. Bake in 375°F oven 30 minutes.

Lean 'n Tasty Divan

4 servings

- 1 package (10 oz.) frozen broccoli spears, thawed
- 1 package (12 oz.) Oscar Mayer "Lean 'n Tasty" breakfast strips
- 1 cup water
- 4 slices process American cheese, cut in half
- 4 servings hot cooked rice
  Toothpicks

Separate broccoli into 8 portions. Wrap 1 or 2 breakfast strips around each portion. Secure with toothpicks. Place in a large skillet. Add water. Cover. Bring to a boil. Turn down heat. Simmer 15 minutes or until broccoli is tender. Remove from heat. Pour off liquid. Remove toothpicks. Place half slice cheese on each portion. Cover and let stand 1 minute. Serve on rice.

Calico Hot Dog Macaroni

4 servings

- 1 package (16 oz.) Oscar Mayer wieners
- 1 package (7 oz.) macaroni
- 1 can (10¾ oz.) cream of celery soup
- 2 medium carrots, shredded
- 1 medium onion, chopped
- ½ green pepper, chopped
- 1 cup (8 oz.) sour cream
- ½ teaspoon dill weed

Set aside 4 wieners; cut remaining wieners into 1-inch pieces. Cook macaroni according to package directions. Combine with wiener pieces and remaining ingredients in 2-quart casserole. Bake in 350°F oven 25 minutes. Top with whole wieners; bake 15 minutes more.

Microwave: Follow directions above, combining ingredients in 2-quart casserole. Cover. Microwave at HIGH 6 to 7 minutes, stirring after three minutes. Stir again. Top with whole wieners. Cover. Microwave at HIGH 5 to 6 minutes more.

Go Fly a Kite!

One way to fly high on a family outing or get a party off the ground is to build your own kite. You can add paint, glitter or crepe paper streamers to a purchased kite or, if you're really ambitious, start from scratch. Get a book from the library on the principles of how a kite works. It'll also give you design ideas. You'll need light strips of balsa wood or plastic tubing (like soda straws) for the frame. Tissue paper or thin plastic (dry cleaner or trash bag) makes the surface. Try Chinese fish kites, box kites, butterflies or airplanes. Start saving those nylon stockings now for the great "tales" that will follow. Up, up and away!

Come Blow Your Horn at a Mardi Gras Party

*T*he New Orleans Mardi Gras is legendary for extravagant fun, festivity and frivolity. The streets are filled with music, color and extravagance.

Create a Mardi Gras on your own street any time of the year. Just organize a block party. Arrange for a New Orleans-type jazz band to play (or Dixieland records will do) and decorate a'la New Orleans' French Quarter. Everyone should wear a mask and a costume. If you have an extremely ambitious group, you can create a float (for the less industrious, ice cream floats will suffice). Crown a king and queen. Toss doubloons. Let everyone pitch in with the food . . . one street ought to produce a lot of interesting dishes. Creole cooking, Gumbo and Jambalaya are musts.

Quick Jambalaya

4 servings

- 1 package (12 oz.) Oscar Mayer "Smokie Links"
- 1 package (8 oz.) Oscar Mayer ham slice, cubed
- 1 can (16 oz.) whole tomatoes, undrained and coarsely chopped
- 1 can (10¾ oz.) chicken broth
- 1 medium green pepper, chopped
- 1 medium onion, chopped
- ½ teaspoon thyme
- 5 drops bottled hot pepper sauce
- 1¾ cups instant rice

Combine all ingredients except rice in large Dutch oven or saucepot. Bring to a boil, stirring occasionally. Stir in rice. Turn down heat. Cover. Simmer 10 minutes until liquid is absorbed.

Wieners Viennese

5 servings

- 2 cups sauerkraut, well-drained
- 1 cup (8 oz.) sour cream
- 1 medium onion, finely chopped
- 3 tablespoons brown sugar
- 1 package (16 oz.) Oscar Mayer wieners

Combine sauerkraut, sour cream, onion and brown sugar in 2-quart baking dish. Top with wieners. Bake in 350°F oven 20 minutes.

Ham Steaks En Crôute

2 servings

- 1 package (8 oz.) Oscar Mayer ham steaks
- 1 can (8 oz.) refrigerated crescent roll dough
- 1 cup sliced cooked sweet potatoes
- ¼ cup orange marmalade
- 2 tablespoons butter, melted
  Sesame seeds

Pat ham steaks dry with paper towel. Separate dough into 4 rectangles. Firmly press perforations to seal. Place 2 on ungreased baking sheet. Place 1 ham steak in center of each. Top with half the sweet potatoes and marmalade. Cover with remaining ham steaks. Place remaining rectangles over ham steaks, stretching dough slightly. Pinch edges to seal. Brush top of dough with butter. Sprinkle with sesame seeds. Bake in 375°F oven 25 to 30 minutes or until golden brown.

Filling variations:

Apple 'n Cheese—apple pie filling and a cheese slice.
Ham 'n Swiss—Swiss cheese spread with mustard.
Spinach Supreme—frozen spinach souffle.
Stuffed Steaks—pork stuffing mix.
Broccoli Cheese Stacks—chopped broccoli with a slice of Cheddar cheese.

Sausage Creole Soup

6 servin

- 1 package (12 oz.) Oscar Maye "Smokie Links"
- ¼ cup butter
- 1 stalk celery, cut into ½-inch pieces
- 1 green pepper, cut into 1-inch pieces
- 1 medium onion, cut into wedg
- 1 can (28 oz.) tomatoes with liquid
- 1 can (6 oz.) tomato juice
- 1 clove garlic, finely chopped
- 1 bay leaf
- ¼ teaspoon pepper
- ¼ teaspoon thyme
- ¼ teaspoon bottled hot pepper sauce

Cut Smokie Links into 1-inch pieces. Melt butter in large saucepan. Add celery, green pepper and onion. Cook and stir on medium-low 10 minutes or until tender-crisp. Add remainin ingredients; stir to break up tomatoes. Bring to a boil. Turn down heat. Cover. Simmer 15 minutes.

Reuben Casserole

4 servin

- 1 package (12 oz.) Oscar Maye "Smokie Links"
- 1 package (7 oz.) macaroni
- 2 cups sauerkraut, drained
- 1½ cups (6 oz.) shredded Swiss cheese
- ½ cup Thousand Island dressin
- 2 slices rye bread, cubed

Cut Smokie Links into 1-inch pieces. Cook macaroni according package directions; drain. Combi all ingredients except bread and cup shredded cheese in 2-quart casserole. Top with bread and reserved cheese. Bake in 350°F oven 40 minutes.

Smokie Cheesie Chowder

4 servings

1 package (12 oz.) Oscar Mayer "Smokie Links"
1 can (10¾ oz.) Cheddar cheese soup
1 can (16 oz.) mixed vegetables with liquid
1 tablespoon instant minced onion

Cut Smokie Links into penny-size pieces. Combine with remaining ingredients in saucepan. Heat about 10 minutes.

Liver, Bacon and Onions

4 servings

slices Oscar Mayer bacon
medium onions, sliced and separated into rings
slices (16 oz.) beef liver
Flour seasoned with pepper

Cook bacon in skillet according to package directions; drain, reserving drippings in skillet. Add onions to skillet. Cook on medium until tender. Push to side of skillet. Coat liver with flour. Cook on medium 8 to 10 minutes, turning to brown both sides. Place cooked liver on platter with onions; top with bacon.

Ribboned Bacon Roll

6 servings

1 package (16 oz.) Oscar Mayer bacon
1 package (6 oz.) chicken flavor stuffing mix
2 stalks celery, chopped
1 small onion, chopped

Gravy:
1 teaspoon instant chicken bouillon
1 cup boiling water
3 tablespoons flour
⅛ teaspoon pepper
½ cup milk

Separate bacon slices and reassemble on waxed paper, overlapping slices ½ inch, to form a sheet of bacon slices measuring 14x9 inches. Prepare stuffing mix according to package directions adding celery and onion. Shape dressing into a roll lengthwise across bacon. Bring bacon up over dressing overlapping the ends of slices. Place bacon roll seam-side down on rack in a shallow baking pan. Bake in 375°F oven 30 minutes or until bacon is crisp. To prepare gravy: Dissolve bouillon in water. Combine 3 tablespoons drippings, flour and seasonings in saucepan. Stir in bouillon mixture and milk. Heat to boiling, stirring constantly. Boil 1 minute. Cut bacon roll into slices. Serve with gravy.

Hot Ham Salad

4 servings

1 package (8 oz.) Oscar Mayer chopped ham
1 package (6 oz.) process American cheese
1½ cups diagonally sliced celery
1½ cups seasoned croutons
1 cup mayonnaise
1 jar (2 oz.) sliced pimientos
¼ cup slivered almonds
1 teaspoon instant minced onion

Cut ham and cheese into 1-inch cubes. Combine all ingredients in large bowl. Spoon into 1½-quart casserole. Bake in 350°F oven for 25 minutes or until cheese is melted.

Microwave: Cut ham and cheese into 1-inch cubes. Combine all ingredients in large bowl. Spoon into 10x6-inch glass baking dish. Cover with waxed paper. Microwave at HIGH 5½ to 6½ minutes stirring after three minutes.

Western Wiener Scallop

4 servings

1 package (16 oz.) Oscar Mayer wieners
1 tablespoon butter
1 can (16 oz.) stewed tomatoes
1 can (16 oz.) whole kernel corn, drained
1 can (6 oz.) tomato paste
½ cup sliced stuffed green olives
½ teaspoon chili powder
½ cup (2 oz.) shredded Cheddar cheese

Cut wieners in half lengthwise, then crosswise. Melt butter in skillet. Add wieners. Cook on medium until browned. Add remaining ingredients except cheese. Cook 10 minutes more, stirring often. Sprinkle with cheese. Continue heating until cheese begins to melt.

The After-Income-Tax-Day Party

Once April 16th rolls around you'll need a party! (The months before are so taxing!) Poverty means using empty juice cans for glasses and wearing tattered clothes from the local thrift shop. Dig up a few extra 1040 forms and make confetti out of 'em! Find some money clips at the five-and-dime store for napkin rings, and use the infamous income tax instructions for placemats. Be sure to have a wealth of food on hand for your penniless friends—try Wieners Olé or Care Package Casserole. Give each guest their own after-dinner "mint" and have plenty of foil-wrapped chocolate coins around to help restore everyone's wealth.

Ham Steaks Au Poivre

2 servings

1 package (8 oz.) Oscar Mayer ham steaks
1 tablespoon cracked black pepper
1 tablespoon butter
1 cup dry white wine
1 teaspoon Dijon mustard
1 teaspoon Worcestershire sauce

Coat both sides of ham steaks with black pepper. Melt butter in large skillet on medium. Brown ham, turning once. Transfer ham to serving platter. Cover. Keep warm. Add wine to skillet. Cook on high 2 minutes or until liquid is reduced to half the volume. Remove from heat. Stir in mustard and Worcestershire sauce. Pour over ham. Serve immediately.
290 calories/serving

Picture This!

*W*ith a little early planning, you can make this anniversary or birthday more memorable than ever. Surprise your special person with a "This Is Your Life" party. A few months before the big day, send out requests to everyone that's played a part in your honored guest's life, from his or her first grade teacher to buddies at summer camp. Ask them to send their good wishes and reminiscent messages to a special address (perhaps a neighbor or relative). Dig out souvenirs from the attic and use high school yearbooks and old photos, along with the cards received, to compile a unique "This Is Your Life" album. An appearance by a special guest (college roommate or favorite cousin) would make the day even more unforgettable. Video tape the surprise party to preserve the memories "happily ever after."

Flaming Ham Slice

2 servings

1 package (8 oz.) Oscar Mayer ham slice
¼ cup brandy

Sauce:
1 lemon
⅓ cup brown sugar
1 tablespoon prepared mustard

Cut lemon in half. Thinly slice one half; grate peel and squeeze juice from other half. Combine juice, peel, brown sugar and mustard in a small bowl. Place ham on broiler pan; broil 4 inches from heat 5 minutes. Turn ham slice. Brush with sauce; top with lemon slices. Broil 5 minutes more. Transfer to platter. Heat brandy in small saucepan until it begins to sizzle around sides of pan when tilted. Remove from heat. Light brandy using long match; pour flaming brandy over ham.
345 calories/serving

Ham, Avocado and Crab Supreme

4 servings

1 package (6 oz.) Oscar Mayer smoked cooked ham
1 can (6 oz.) crab meat, drained
2 English muffins, split
1 avocado
Lemon juice
4 slices process American cheese

Place two slices ham and ¼ of the crab on each muffin half. Place in 9-inch square glass baking dish. Peel avocado; cut into 12 wedges. Dip in lemon juice to prevent discoloring. Arrange on crab. Bake in 350°F oven 15 minutes. Top each with cheese. Bake 2 minutes more or until cheese melts.

Microwave: Assemble as above. Cover with wax paper. Microwave at HIGH 4 minutes, rotating dish after two minutes. Top each with cheese. Microwave 30 seconds more or until cheese melts.

Bacon Jardin

2 servin...

10 slices Oscar Mayer bacon
¾ cup instant rice
¾ cup boiling water
1 small zucchini, sliced
¼ teaspoon oregano
1 tomato, sliced
1 small onion, sliced
1 green pepper, sliced into ring
4 slices American process cheese, cut diagonally

Cut bacon into 1-inch pieces. Co... in skillet on medium-low until crisp; pour off drippings. Stir in rice, water and zucchini. Sprinkle with oregano. Top with tomato, onion and green pepper. Cover. Simmer 10 minutes or until vegetables are tender-crisp. Top with cheese. Cover. Heat just un... cheese begins to melt.

Easy Canneloni

5 servin...

5 lasagna noodles, cooked
2 packages (8 oz. each) Oscar Mayer cotto salami
10 slices mozzarella cheese, eac... approximately 4x2 inches
1 jar (15½ oz.) spaghetti sauce
¼ cup grated Parmesan cheese

Cut noodles in half crosswise. Place 2 slices meat and 1 strip cheese on each. Roll; place seam side down in 9-inch square glass baking dish. Top with spaghetti sauce; sprinkle with cheese. Bak... in 350°F oven 30 minutes or unt... hot and bubbly.

Microwave: Assemble as above except for Parmesan cheese. Cov... with waxed paper. Microwave at HIGH 15 to 16 minutes, rotating dish twice during heating. Sprin... with Parmesan cheese. Let stand covered 5 minutes.

Ham Veronique

2 servings

1 tablespoon butter
⅓ cup dry white wine
1 can (8 oz.) seedless grapes, with liquid*
1 tablespoon lemon juice
2 teaspoons cornstarch
1 package (8 oz.) Oscar Mayer ham slice

Melt butter in large skillet. Add wine, grapes, lemon juice and cornstarch; blend well. Bring to a boil on medium, stirring constantly. Push grapes aside and add ham. Cover. Simmer about 5 minutes.
285 calories/serving

*Or use ¾ cup fresh seedless grapes (about ¼ lb.), ⅓ cup water and 1 tablespoon sugar.

Health Spa Soup

4 servings

1 package (8 oz.) Oscar Mayer peppered ham
2 cans (10¾ oz. each) chicken broth
3 cups water
1 medium onion, chopped
1 cup (3 oz.) sliced fresh mushrooms
⅓ cup quick-cooking barley
¼ cup chopped fresh parsley
1 small bunch (12 oz.) escarole or romaine
4 teaspoons grated Parmesan cheese

Cut stacked meat into 1-inch cubes; set aside. Combine broth, water, onion, mushrooms, barley and parsley in Dutch oven. Bring to a boil. Turn down heat. Cover. Simmer 10 minutes. Tear escarole into bite-size pieces. Add escarole and meat. Cover. Simmer 5 minutes more. Serve in bowls. Sprinkle with Parmesan cheese just before serving.
235 calories/serving

Bacon Florentine Shells

4 servings

1 package (16 oz.) Oscar Mayer bacon
1 package (10 to 12 oz.) jumbo shell macaroni
1 package (10 oz.) frozen chopped spinach, thawed
1 package (8 oz.) cream cheese
1 egg

Sauce:

1 small onion, chopped
1 can (16 oz.) stewed tomatoes
1 can (8 oz.) tomato sauce

Cut bacon into ½-inch pieces. Cook in skillet on medium-low until crisp. Remove bacon, reserving 1 tablespoon drippings. Meanwhile cook shells according to package directions; rinse in cold water. Place spinach in colander. Press to remove excess moisture. Combine spinach, cream cheese, egg and half of bacon pieces in bowl; blend well. Fill each shell with 1 tablespoon bacon-spinach mixture. Place shells in 2-quart casserole. Cook onion in reserved drippings. Add tomatoes and tomato sauce. Bring to a boil. Pour over shells. Sprinkle with remaining bacon. Cover. Bake in 350°F oven 40 minutes.

To Make Ahead: Assemble as above. Cover and refrigerate. Bake in 350°F oven 1 hour.

Baked Ruby-Fruited Ham

12 servings

1 can (3 lbs.) Oscar Mayer ham
¼ cup brown sugar
2 teaspoons cornstarch
1 can (8 oz.) jellied cranberry sauce
3 kumquats, sliced, optional
¼ cup Burgundy wine
⅛ teaspoon ground cloves

Bake ham according to package directions. Meanwhile, combine sugar and cornstarch in saucepan. Stir in remaining ingredients. Bring to a boil. Turn down heat. Simmer 10 minutes. Brush on ham last 30 minutes of baking time. Serve remainder as sauce.
185 calories/serving

Surprise Popovers

6 popovers

10 slices Oscar Mayer bacon
2 eggs
1 cup milk
1 cup flour

Cut bacon into ½-inch pieces. Cook in large skillet on medium-low until crisp; drain. Combine eggs, milk and flour in bowl. Beat just until smooth. Stir in bacon. Pour into 6 (6 oz.) well-greased custard cups. Place on shallow baking pan for easier handling. Bake in 450°F oven 20 minutes. Decrease oven temperature to 350°F; bake 15 minutes more. Serve with butter or honey.

Fortune Telling Fest

Will you be going on a long trip? Is Mr. Right right around the corner? No one would admit to doing it on their own, but plenty of people would get a kick out of getting their palms read ... seeing how the tarot cards fall ... hearing from the crystal ball. You probably have a local psychic who would come for a few hours and provide some unique fun.

Decorate with a gypsy flair, candles and astrology charts. Your invitations can be a picture of a crystal ball saying "I see a party in your future."

Ham
Apricot Crepes

4 servings

1 package (6 oz.) Oscar Mayer
  smoked cooked ham
8 crepes*
1 can (8¾ oz.) apricot halves
2 tablespoons cornstarch
2 tablespoons brown sugar
1 can (12 oz.) apricot nectar
2 tablespoons butter
1 tablespoon lemon juice

oll ham slices in crepes. Place in
-inch square baking dish. Drain
pricots, reserving liquid. Place
pricots in pan with ham crepes.
lake sauce by mixing cornstarch
ith brown sugar in saucepan. Add
eserved apricot liquid and apricot
ectar. Cook on medium stirring
onstantly until thickened.
emove from heat; stir in butter
nd lemon juice. Pour over crepes.
ake in 400°F oven 15 minutes.

o *Flame:* Heat 2 tablespoons rum
 small saucepan until it begins to
zzle around sides of pan when
ted. Remove from heat. Light
m using a long match; pour
ming rum over crepes.

Crepes:

3 eggs, beaten
¼ cup flour
¼ cup milk
¼ teaspoon salt
2 tablespoons butter, melted

ombine eggs, flour, milk and salt
 medium bowl. Brush bottom of
inch skillet (use a skillet with
rved sides or a French crepe
n) with butter. Heat on
edium-high. Skillet is ready
en a drop of water sizzles. Pour
to 3 tablespoons batter in pan.
uickly lift pan from heat and
irl until batter covers bottom of
n in a thin film. Return pan to
at for about 1 minute, until
ttom of crepe is brown. Loosen
th spatula; turn and brown other
de for about 30 seconds. Place on
per towel. Repeat.

Ham Gateau

6 servings

2 packages (6 oz. each) Oscar
  Mayer smoked cooked ham
1 package (8 oz.) sliced natural
  Swiss cheese
8 crepes*

Sauce:

1 can (10¾ oz.) cream of
  mushroom soup
½ cup milk
¼ cup white wine

Filling:

1 small onion, chopped
1 tablespoon butter
2 packages (10 oz. each) frozen
  chopped broccoli
2 cans (4 oz. each) mushroom
  stems and pieces, drained

Combine sauce ingredients in
saucepan. Heat on medium. Cover;
remove from heat. Cook onions in
butter in large skillet until tender.
Add broccoli and mushrooms.
Cover. Cook 10 minutes. Stir in ½
cup sauce. Stack gateau in shallow
pan as follows: 1 crepe, ¼ broccoli
mixture, 1 crepe, 1 slice cheese, 4
slices ham. Repeat 3 times. Top
with remaining crepe and cheese.
Pour ½ cup sauce over gateau.
Bake in 350°F oven 40 minutes.
Heat remaining sauce. Cut gateau
into wedges. Serve with sauce.

*for crepe recipe see Ham Apricot Crepes

*I*magine the life of a world
traveler . . . inviting friends
onto your yacht at each new
port of call . . . hosting yet
another international party.
Well you may not have the
yacht, but who says you can't
captain an international tour!

*Choose the countries you'd like
to "visit." Make invitations
look like passports or cruise
tickets. Get each guest involved
by bringing a dish (appetizer,
salad or dessert) from one of
the countries listed on the
"itinerary." Or move the party
from home to home as you
"travel around the world" in a
single evening.*

*Decorate with posters (from
your travel agent) portraying
some of the picturesque villages
and scenery you'll see on your
cruise. Provide authentic music
and greet your friends
appropriately (Hola, Ciao or
Bonjour) before you set sail.
Crack open the champagne,
throw confetti and . . . Bon
Voyage!*

Souffle-Topped
Ham Slice

2 servings

1 package (8 oz.) Oscar Mayer
  ham slice

Topping:

1 egg, separated
1 cup (4 oz.) shredded Cheddar
  cheese
¼ teaspoon baking powder
2 tablespoons sliced olives

Beat egg white until stiff. Combine
cheese, egg yolk, baking powder
and olives in another bowl. Fold in
beaten egg white. Place ham slice
on broiler pan. Broil 4 inches from
heat 5 minutes. Turn ham slice
and spread with topping. Broil 1½
minutes more or until topping is
puffed and lightly browned.

Cold Cut Pizza

8 servings

1 package (8 oz.) Oscar Mayer cotto salami
1 package (8 oz.) refrigerated crescent roll dough
1 package (8 oz.) cream cheese, softened
½ teaspoon dill weed
¼ teaspoon garlic powder
1 cup alfalfa sprouts
3 green onions, chopped
1 medium tomato, sliced
1 small cucumber, sliced

Cut meat into quarters; set aside. Generously grease 12 to 14-inch pizza pan. Separate dough into triangles; arrange spoke-fashion in pan with pointed ends toward center to cover bottom of pan. Press edges of triangles together sealing to form crust. Bake in 375°F oven about 8 minutes until golden brown. Cool. Combine cream cheese, dill weed and garlic powder. Spread over crust. Top with alfalfa sprouts and onion. Arrange meat and vegetables on top. Cut into wedges to serve.
300 calories/serving

Barbecued Ham Sandwiches

24 sandwiches

1 can (3 lb.) Oscar Mayer ham
24 round sandwich buns

Sauce:
1 bottle (14 oz.) catsup (about 1⅓ cups)
1 medium onion, finely chopped
1 medium green pepper, chopped
¼ cup butter
⅓ cup brown sugar
⅓ cup prepared mustard
1 tablespoon Worcestershire sauce

Slice ham as thin as possible; layer in 13x9-inch pan. Combine sauce ingredients in saucepan. Simmer 15 minutes, stirring occasionally. Pour over ham. Bake uncovered in 350°F oven 40 minutes. Serve in buns, allowing 2 to 3 slices for each sandwich.
200 calories/sandwich

The Team Hero

20 sandwiche

1 package (1 lb.) frozen wheat o pumpernickel bread dough
1 package (1 lb.) frozen white bread dough
   Butter
   Lettuce leaves
4 large tomatoes, thinly sliced
1 large onion, thinly sliced and separated into rings
3 packages (8 oz. each) Oscar Mayer ham and cheese loaf
3 packages (8 oz. each) Oscar Mayer New England brand sausage
1 bottle (8 oz.) creamy Italian dressing

Thaw bread dough according to package directions. Stretch each loaf into a 20 to 24-inch rope. Twist one wheat rope and one white rope together. Lay diagonally across greased baking sheet. Repeat to form second twis Cover dough and let rise in warm place until doubled in size, about hours. Bake in 375°F oven 20 to 25 minutes. Brush with melted butter. Cool; slice in half lengthwise. Layer bottom half of loaf with lettuce, tomato, onion rings and meat. Spread ½ cup dressing on cut surface of top ha of bread. Place over meat layer. Repeat with remaining ingredient to form second hero sandwich. C each hero into 10 servings.

Team Up for a Super Bowl Party

Y ou can be the M.V.P. at this year's Super Bowl when you invite your friends over for a "Super Sunday" party. With just a little pre-game planning the party will run smoothly, and you'll be able to spend the big day with your guests, cheering on your favorite team.

Make your invitations look like football tickets. Give the "game plan" inside. Let your guests

know it's a party they can't "pass" up. Decorate your party room with pennants and ask your friends to dress in the colors of their projected winner. Play rah-rah marching music on the stereo to kick off the game as you bring in the chips

Half-time activities can include a preplanned football trivia quiz, along with plenty of popcorn, peanuts and hot dogs for the hungry fans.

Making Pizza Makes the Party

Why order out for that same ol' pizza pie when it's much more fun to create "designer" pizzas at home. You provide the crusts and a spicy Italian sauce; ask each guest to bring a favorite ingredient. Suggest standbys like mozzarella cheese, pepperoni, bacon bits and mushrooms. Include some more exotic fare like black olives, anchovies, Canadian bacon and sauerkraut. Arrange a smorgasbord and let each guest create a custom-made Italian masterpiece!

Decorate your pizzeria with red-checkered tablecloths and candles in wine bottles. Set out grated cheese and oregano for those pizza connoisseurs. A great big tossed salad will be welcomed by the extra-hungry. Pour plenty of soda pop and . . . you've got pizza pizzazz!

Baked Jubilee Ham with Spicy Cherry Sauce

12 servings

1 can (3 lb.) Oscar Mayer ham
1 can (1 lb. 5 oz.) cherry pie filling
⅛ teaspoon cinnamon
⅛ teaspoon ground cloves

Bake ham according to package directions. Combine pie filling, cinnamon and cloves in saucepan. Bring to a boil. Turn down heat. Simmer 5 minutes. Brush on ham last 30 minutes of baking time. Serve remainder as sauce.
190 calories/serving

Bacon Crunch Snack Bars

24 bars

1 cup chunk-style peanut butter
⅓ cup honey
1 can (3 oz.) Oscar Mayer bacon bits
2 cups grape-nuts cereal

Combine peanut butter and honey in large saucepan. Heat stirring occasionally on medium-low until mixture bubbles. Remove from heat. Stir in bacon and cereal. Press firmly into buttered 9-inch square pan. Chill at least 1 hour. Cut into bars.
120 calories/serving

Microwave: Combine peanut butter and honey in 2-quart glass mixing bowl. Microwave at HIGH 2 to 2½ minutes just until mixture bubbles, stirring after one minute. Stir in bacon and cereal. Press firmly into buttered 9-inch square pan. Chill at least 1 hour.

Pasta Primavera

8 servings

2 packages (6 oz. each) Oscar Mayer smoked cooked ham
1 bag (16 oz.) frozen mixed vegetables
½ cup butter
1 teaspoon basil leaves
½ teaspoon garlic powder
1 package (16 oz.) medium noodles, cooked
1 cup (8 oz.) sour cream

Cut ham into 1-inch pieces. Combine ham, vegetables, ¼ cup butter, basil and ¼ teaspoon garlic in large skillet. Heat on medium 10 minutes until vegetables are tender-crisp, stirring occasionally. Toss noodles with remaining butter, garlic and sour cream. Place noodles on serving platter. Top with ham mixture.
325 calories/serving

Lemon Frosted Ham

12 serving

1 can (3 lbs.) Oscar Mayer ham
1 package (8 oz.) cream cheese
½ cup lemon flavored yogurt
1 teaspoon prepared horseradi
  Lemon slices
  Cucumber slices

Place ham on serving platter. Combine cream cheese, yogurt an horseradish in bowl; beat until smooth. Spread mixture over top and sides of ham. Cover; chill several hours or overnight. Garni with lemon and cucumber slices just before serving.
215 calories/serving

Note: Insert toothpicks into sides and to of ham before covering with plastic wrap foil.

Four Layer Feast

8 servin

Slice a large round loaf (1½ lbs.) of cracked wheat, light or dark ry bread horizontally into four layer Spread each layer with butter, mayonnaise or spicy mustard. Assemble as follows:

Bottom layer: Leaf lettuce, 2 packages (6 oz. each) Oscar Mayer smoked cooked ham, ½ lb. sliced Swiss cheese.

Middle layer: 1 package (8 oz.) Oscar Mayer hard salami and ½ lb. (1 cup) coleslaw.

Top layer: Leaf lettuce, ½ lb. thi sliced turkey, tomato slices and sliced onion.

Close sandwich with top crust. Insert 8 long skewers through to crust to bottom of sandwich. Garnish each skewer with cherry tomatoes, olives, pickles or cockt onions. Cut sandwich between skewers into 8 wedges.

Food for A Crowd

Trying to figure out how much food to fix for a crowd can be confusing. How much you need depends on what you are serving. Generally, plan on 1½ to 2 sandwiches and 2 servings of salads or baked beans per person. Here's our handy guide to help you in planning.

Number of People	Cold Cuts 3 oz./ Person (1)	Cheese 1½ oz./ Person	Bread 3 Slices/ Person (2)	Chips/ Snacks 1½ oz./ Person	Dip 3 Tbsp./ Person	Hot Dogs 2/Person (3)	Rolls or Buns 2/Person	Baked Ham 4 oz./ Person	Salads (Potato, Coleslaw, Baked Beans) ¾ Cup/ Person	Ice Cream ¾ Cup/ Person	Cookies 2/Person	Cold Drinks 18 oz. or 3-6 oz. Cups/ Person	Hot Drinks 2 Cups/ Person (4)
12	2¼ lbs. 5 pkgs.	1¼ lbs.	2 loaves	1 lb.	2¼ cups	2½ lbs. 3 pkgs.	2 doz.	3 lbs.	2¼ qts.	2¼ qts.	2 doz.	6¾ qts.	1.5 gal. (½ lb.)
20	3¾ lbs. 8 pkgs.	2 lbs.	3 loaves	2 lbs.	3¾ cups	4 lbs. 4 pkgs.	3½ doz.	5 lbs.	3¾ qts.	3¾ gal.	3½ doz.	3 gal.	2.5 gal. (¾ lb.)
35	6½ lbs. 13 pkgs.	3¼ lbs.	5¼ loaves	3¼ lbs.	6½ cups	7 lbs. 7 pkgs.	5½ doz.	8¾ lbs.	1¾ gal.	1¾ gal.	5½ doz.	5 gal.	4½ gal. (2 lbs.)
50	9½ lbs. 19 pkgs.	4¾ lbs.	7½ loaves	4¾ lbs.	9½ cups	10 lbs. 10 pkgs.	8½ doz.	12½ lbs.	2½ gal.	2½ gal.	8½ doz.	7 gal.	6¼ gal. (2½ lbs.)
65	12 lbs. 24 pkgs.	6 lbs.	9¾ loaves	6 lbs.	12 cups	13 lbs. 13 pkgs.	11 doz.	16½ lbs.	3 gal.	3 gal.	11 doz.	9 gal.	8 gal. (3 lbs.)

1) # of packages based on Oscar Mayer 8 oz. units—8 to 10 slices per package
2) Bread based on 20 slices per loaf
3) Hot dogs based on 10 links per pound
4) Coffee and tea listed in pounds

Baked Beans for a Crowd

25 servings

1 package (1 lb.) Oscar Mayer bacon
2 medium onions, chopped
7 cans (1 lb. each) baked beans or 1 No. 10 can baked beans
1 cup brown sugar
¼ cup molasses
2 tablespoons Worcestershire sauce
½ teaspoons dry mustard

ut bacon into 1-inch pieces. Cook 5-quart Dutch oven on edium-low until crisp. Add maining ingredients. Heat 20 inutes on medium, stirring casionally.

Make Ahead: Prepare as above but do t heat. Cover and refrigerate several urs or overnight. Bake covered in 325°F en 2 hours.

It's Easy to Get "Up" for a Hoe-Down

Got a big rec room, patio or nearby park pavilion? Maybe an authentic barn? Have a foot-stompin', fun-rompin' barn dance. Folk dancing is easy to learn and easy to love. All you need is space, guests and a lively caller. It's great for couples or singles, 'cause you end up dancing with just about everybody. Decorating means dragging in bales of hay to sit on, stuffing a scarecrow and possibly painting a backdrop of a big red barn, complete with silo and hay loft. Have a few shocks of corn and pumpkins around if they're in season. Ask the fellas to come in overalls and plaid shirts. Gals should wear flat shoes and full skirts. The food is easy and in the mood ... Barbecued Ham Sandwiches, Speedy Baked Beans and Bacony Cole Slaw.

On a smaller scale, you could just invite three other couples over to your place, get some instructional square dance records and teach yourselves one evening. Then you'll be right in step when someone ELSE throws a big party.

Gift Wrapped Ham

12 servings

1 can (3 lbs.) Oscar Mayer ham
1 sheet frozen puff pastry, thawed
1 teaspoon dry mustard
½ teaspoon sage
1 egg, beaten
Raisin Wine Sauce*

Place ham on foil-lined shallow baking pan. Pat dry to absorb extra moisture. Sprinkle with mustard and sage. Wrap ham in pastry, folding ends like a package. Use water to seal seams. Brush pastry with egg. Bake in 375°F oven 1 hour 20 minutes. Serve with Raisin Wine Sauce.

Note: Three unbaked pie crusts can be used in place of puff pastry. Wrap ham; bake 1 hour in 400°F oven.

Raisin Wine Sauce:
¼ cup sugar
3 tablespoons cornstarch
1 teaspoon dry mustard
1 cup dry red wine
½ cup water
½ cup seedless raisins
1 jar (10 oz.) currant jelly

Combine ingredients except jelly in saucepan. Cook, stirring constantly, on medium-low 5 minutes or until sauce thickens and boils. Stir in jelly. Heat 3 minutes more or until jelly melts.

Savory Bacon Dip

1 can (3 oz.) Oscar Mayer bacon bits*
1 cup (8 oz.) sour cream
1 tablespoon instant minced onion
1 tablespoon prepared mustard
2 teaspoons steak sauce

Set aside 1 tablespoon bacon bits for garnish. Combine bacon bits with remaining ingredients; mix well. Cover. Chill 1 hour. Garnish with reserved bacon bits.

*or use 10 slices Oscar Mayer bacon, cooked and crumbled

Gift Wrapped Ham

Party
Sandwich Loaf

14 servings

1 loaf (1½ lb.) unsliced bread
1 package (8 oz.) Oscar Mayer braunschweiger liver sausage
1 cup egg salad*
1 package (8 oz.) Oscar Mayer sandwich spread
1 package (8 oz.) Oscar Mayer ham and cheese spread
1 container (12 oz.) spreadable cream cheese
Chopped fresh parsley

Trim all crusts from bread. Cut loaf lengthwise into 4 layers. Spread first layer with braunschweiger topped with egg salad, second layer sandwich spread, third layer ham and cheese spread. Close sandwich with fourth layer. Frost top and sides with cream cheese and garnish with parsley. To serve, cut loaf into ½-inch slices.

Note: An electric knife works well to trim and slice bread.

Egg Salad:
2 hard-cooked eggs, chopped
6 ripe olives, chopped
¼ cup mayonnaise
1 tablespoon chopped onion
Salt
Pepper

Combine ingredients.

ABC Appetizers

24 appetizers

1 can (3 oz.) Oscar Mayer bacon bits
2 cups corn chips, crushed
½ cup mayonnaise
¼ teaspoon chili powder
1 avocado
Toothpicks

Combine bacon bits and corn chips in shallow bowl. Mix together mayonnaise and chili powder in another bowl. Peel avocado; cut into chunks. Pierce each chunk with toothpick. Dip into mayonnaise mixture, then coat with bacon bits mixture. Refrigerate until ready to serve.

Spinach Supreme

6 servings

10 slices Oscar Mayer bacon
2 packages (10 oz. each) frozen chopped spinach
1 cup (8 oz.) sour cream
½ envelope dry onion soup mix (about 2 tablespoons)

Cut bacon into 1-inch pieces. Cook in skillet on medium-low until crisp; drain. Cook spinach; drain well. Stir in bacon, sour cream and soup mix. Heat on medium-low 5 minutes.

Microwave: Cut bacon into 1-inch pieces. Place in 10x7-inch glass baking dish; cover with paper towel. Microwave at HIGH 7 to 9 minutes until crisp, stirring twice with 2 forks to separate pieces. Drain. Place spinach in 1½ quart glass casserole. Cover. Microwave at HIGH 9 minutes, stirring once. Drain well. Stir in bacon, sour cream and soup mix. Cover. Microwave at HIGH 6 to 7 minutes, stirring once.

Braunschweiger
Herb Stuffing

6 servings

1 package (4 oz.) Oscar Mayer braunschweiger liver sausage
1 package (6 oz.) chicken stuffing mix
1 medium onion, chopped
2 stalks celery, chopped
¼ cup butter
1½ cups hot water

Combine braunschweiger, stuffing mix with seasoning packet, onion, celery, butter and water in large bowl. Place stuffing in a 2-quart casserole dish. Bake in 350°F oven 30 minutes.

240 calories/serving

Note: Makes 4 cups stuffing—enough for 6 to 8 Cornish game hens or a 12-pound turkey.

O, Tannenbaum

The first American Christmas tree was put up by German immigrants in Pennsylvania in 1821. Decorated lavishly with fruits and nuts, cookies, dolls, ribbons and painted egg shells, it was such a unique attraction that people paid 6½¢ to see it!

Invite your friends to an old-fashioned tree trimming party for the mere admission fee of one homemade ornament. Place a Yule log on the hearth and hang mistletoe in the doorways. Provide cranberries and popcorn to string, colorful ribbons to tie on the branches, and cookies—to hang and to eat! Forget about commercial ornaments, tinsel and flashing electric lights.

Serve a hot, spicy Wassail Bowl of punch (Wassail means "be of good health"), and flame the plum pudding. Have lots of great snacks like our Holiday Dip and the Christmas Meat Tree. Then sit back with your friends and admire your handiwork. Later on, pass out the caroling books and sing holiday favorites like "O Tannenbaum" and that German classic—"Stille Nacht" (which, incidentally, was first performed on a guitar, as a church mouse had eaten through the pump organ's bellows on Christmas Eve). As your guests leave, be of good cheer—have Kris Kringle hand out small gifts like little wooden ornaments or chocolate-covered lebkuchen.

Braunschweiger Holiday Dip

24 servings

2   packages (8 oz. each) Oscar Mayer braunschweiger liver sausage
1   cup (8 oz.) sour cream or plain yogurt
2   teaspoons dill weed
1   jar (24 oz.) kosher pickle slices
1   jar (32 oz.) kosher pickle halves
    Cherry tomatoes, olives, carrots, celery and other fresh vegetables
    Fresh chopped parsley

Combine braunschweiger, sour cream and dill in bowl; blend until smooth. Shape into a triangle on large tray or serving platter. Decorate as shown to resemble Christmas tree. (The garland is made of pickle slices; the tree trunk is a pickle half.) Sprinkle with parsley. Use fresh vegetables and pickles to dip into tree.

Crunchy Ham Cheese Loaves

6 servings

1   package (8 oz.) Oscar Mayer ham and cheese spread
3   French rolls, sliced and buttered

Spread ham and cheese spread on rolls. Place on foil-lined baking sheet. Bake in 400°F oven 15 minutes or until cheese bubbles and bread is crusty. Serve warm.

Holiday Meat Tree

Oscar Mayer cold cuts (bologna, salami, ham, etc.)
Cream cheese
Almonds
Olives and pickles
Cherry tomatoes
Styrofoam cone
Curly endive
Toothpicks
Fancy picks

Create meat ornaments, securing with fancy picks; refrigerate until ready to use.

Bells: Cut round meat slices in half. Form into cone shapes. Insert cherry tomatoes, radishe[s], mushrooms, water chestnuts or ripe olives.

Cubes: Spread cream cheese between 4 square meat slices. Chill; cut into cubes.

Pinwheels: Place 2 square meat slices side by side; spread with cream cheese. Roll to form log. Chill and slice.

Rolls: Cut square meat slices in half. Wrap around small pickle spears.

Wedges: Stack round meat slices cut into wedges.

Roll cream cheese into 1-inch ba[lls]. Insert almonds to resemble star burst. Chill until ready to place [on] top of tree. Cover entire surface [of] styrofoam cone with endive, securing with toothpicks. Decora[te] tree with meat ornaments. Place star burst on top. Arrange tree o[n] platter. Surround with additiona[l] meat ornaments.

Stuffed Zucchini with Bacon

2 servings

5 slices Oscar Mayer bacon
1 medium zucchini
1 green onion, chopped
¼ cup chopped tomato
½ slice bread, torn into small pieces
⅛ teaspoon pepper
2 tablespoons shredded Cheddar cheese

Cook bacon in skillet on medium-low until crisp. Drain; reserve 1 tablespoon drippings. Crumble bacon. Cut zucchini in half lengthwise; scoop out pulp leaving ¼-inch shell. Chop pulp. Combine bacon, pulp, onion, tomato and bread with 1 tablespoon bacon drippings in bowl. Place zucchini shells in 10x6-inch glass baking dish. Stuff shells with mixture. Top with cheese. Cover with foil. Bake in 350°F oven 45 minutes or until tender.
120 calories/serving

Microwave: Place bacon on bacon rack. Microwave at HIGH 4 minutes. Proceed as above, covering with plastic wrap instead of foil. Microwave at HIGH 7 minutes or until tender.

White Wine Glaze for Ham

12 servings

1 can (3 lb.) Oscar Mayer ham

Glaze:

1 envelope unflavored gelatin
1 cup dry white wine or white grape juice

Garnish:

1 small bunch red grapes
1 small green pepper

Blot ham with paper towel to absorb excess moisture; place on rack in shallow pan. Cut grapes in half and seed. Carve stems and leaves from green pepper. Arrange grape halves on top of ham to form cluster; add green pepper stems and leaves. Heat wine in small saucepan until hot but not boiling. Combine gelatin and hot wine, stirring to completely dissolve. Coat ham by spooning ⅓ cup wine mixture across top and down sides of ham. Chill ham 30 minutes. Leave wine mixture at room temperature while chilling ham. Coat ham 2 more times at 30-minute intervals, using remaining mixture. After the last coat, transfer ham to serving platter and cover with plastic wrap. (Toothpicks may be used to suspend plastic wrap and prevent sticking to the gelatin glaze.) Refrigerate until ready to serve.
160 calories/serving

Note: Excess gelatin may be cut into small cubes and used on the serving platter as garnish. This recipe can be prepared a day in advance and refrigerated until serving time.

Terrine of Sausage

32 appetizers

1 package (12 oz.) Oscar Mayer "Little Friers" pork sausage
10 slices Oscar Mayer bacon
1½ pounds fresh ground pork
5 cans (5 oz. each) boned chicken
1 large onion, finely chopped
½ cup whipping cream
¼ cup sherry, optional
2 eggs
¼ cup flour
1½ teaspoons salt
½ teaspoon ginger
½ teaspoon nutmeg
¼ teaspoon cloves
3 bay leaves
8 whole peppercorns
   French bread, sliced

Cook Little Friers according to package directions. Drain. Line sides and bottom of 9x5-inch loaf pan with strips of bacon, extending slices about 2 inches over rim. Combine ground pork, chicken, onion, cream, sherry, eggs, flour, salt, ginger, nutmeg and cloves in large bowl. Mix well. Spoon half of mixture into bacon-lined pan. Arrange cooked sausage links lengthwise over meat mixture. Spoon remaining meat mixture over links; fold bacon strips over filling. Arrange bay leaves and peppercorns on top. Cover pan with foil. Place in a larger pan to catch juices. Bake in 350°F oven 2½ hours. Cool slightly and remove from pan. Chill thoroughly before serving. Cut into thin slices. Serve with French bread.

They'll Owl Have a Hoot at This Halloween Party

If your ghosts and goblins are too old or it's too cold for trick-or-treating, you can have a hair-raising Halloween at home. *Send simple ghost-shaped invitations and write "be my 'ghost' at a Halloween Party."*

Hold a costume contest. Carve pumpkins. Bake pumpkin seeds with salt. Dunk for apples, "pin the tail on the black cat" and tell spooky stories in the dark.

Serve Savory Bacon Dip in a hollowed-out squash. Arrange a cold cut platter for fast sandwich fixin's. Decorate with cobwebs made of gauze strips and turn the lights eerily low. Hang a glow-in-the-dark skeleton on the wall and serve "witches brew" punch.

Speedy Baked Beans with Wieners

6 servings

- 0 slices Oscar Mayer bacon
- 3 cans (1 lb. each) baked beans
- 1 medium onion, chopped
- ¼ cup brown sugar
- 1 tablespoon molasses
- 2 teaspoons Worcestershire sauce
- ½ teaspoon dry mustard
- 1 package (16 oz.) Oscar Mayer wieners

Cut bacon into 1-inch pieces. Cook in skillet on medium-low heat until crisp. Add remaining ingredients. Heat 15 minutes more.

Microwave: Cut bacon into 1-inch pieces. Place in 2-quart glass casserole; cover with paper towel. Microwave 7 to 9 minutes or until crisp, stirring twice with 2 forks to separate pieces. Add onions; cover with paper towel. Microwave at HIGH 2 minutes or until tender. Add remaining ingredients; cover. Microwave at HIGH 8 minutes, stirring halfway through heating.

Ham Sticks Hawaiian

16 sandwiches

- 1 can (3 lb.) Oscar Mayer ham (oblong)
  Hawaiian Sauce*
- 16 hot dog buns

Cut ham lengthwise into 4 equal slices. Cut each slice lengthwise into 4 sticks. Place on shallow baking pan. Brush with Hawaiian Sauce. Bake in 350°F oven 20 to 25 minutes until bubbling. Or, broil 5 inches from heat 3 minutes; turn. Broil 3 to 5 minutes more. Serve in buns.
255 calories/serving

*Hawaiian Sauce:
- 1 can (8 oz.) crushed pineapple with liquid
- ½ cup brown sugar
- 2 tablespoons sugar
- 1 tablespoon vinegar
- 1 tablespoon cornstarch
- ⅛ teaspoon cinnamon
- ⅛ teaspoon cloves

Combine all ingredients in saucepan. Cook on medium stirring constantly until mixture thickens and boils.

Nutrition Wheels

For a picnic or a bike hike, wrap sandwiches in plastic wrap and pack with well-chilled beverages to keep cold.

8 sandwiches

- 1 package (8 oz.) cream cheese, softened
- 2 large carrots, shredded
- ¼ cup raisins
- 1 package (8 oz.) Oscar Mayer honey loaf
- 8 round buns

Combine cream cheese, carrots and raisins. Place meat slices end to end forming one long strip. Spread cream cheese mixture evenly on entire strip. Beginning at one end, roll up making sure meat slices remain next to each other. Wrap and chill 2 hours or overnight. Cut into ½-inch slices. Serve on buns.
220 calories/serving

Grilled Super Sub

Prepare Hearty Hot Hero from page 22. Wrap in foil. Grill 4 inches from coals 20 minutes or until cheese melts, turning frequently.

Get Things Rolling With a Bicycle Picnic

*O*ver 100 million of us have bicycles. Surely you can put together a guest list out of that crowd who'd like to celebrate with a spin and a picnic.

Send invitations on a map of the bike route you're planning. Gear it to your group's experience level and the local terrain. Start from the same point or meet at the picnic grounds on your own. Take your goodies, like Nutrition Wheels, in backpacks and baskets, or have the supplies

driven in (along with a medicine kit, tire pump and a few tools . . . just in case). Easier yet, take the tour and wind up in your own backyard.

Have at least one thermos of piping hot coffee waiting, and another filled with freshly squeezed orange juice. Set out the Ham and Fruit Flan or a tray of sliced meats and cheese. Don't forget to include lots of fresh fruit—like strawberries to dip in sour cream and brown sugar. It's a meal you'll want to linger over, so start cycling early to work up an appetite!

Speedy Baked Beans with
Cheese Hot Dogs

Picturesque Picnic

Plan a romantic picnic for two just like the one you've always dreamed about. Fill your wicker basket with green grapes, apple slices, hard salami and cheese. Tuck in a loaf of French bread and a bottle of wine. Pick some violets or daisies for the centerpiece of your red-and-white checked tablecloth. Choose an idyllic spot and make a day of it . . . wade along the shore . . . pick wild blueberries for dessert.

If you can't escape to the countryside, plan a rooftop picnic at dusk. Take in the summer breeze, city lights . . . and dream on.

Camper's Wiener Stew

4 servings

1 package (16 oz.) Oscar Mayer wieners
1 can (10¾ oz.) vegetable soup
1 can (16 oz.) whole white potatoes, drained and quartered
1 can (16 oz.) sliced carrots, drained
1 can (5½ oz.) tomato juice
¼ teaspoon thyme

Cut wieners into 1-inch pieces. Combine with remaining ingredients in saucepan. Bring to a boil. Cover. Turn down heat. Simmer 10 minutes.

Chili Bean Skillet

No mixing or measuring . . . combine and heat over a campfire or cookstove.

4 servings

1 package (16 oz.) Oscar Mayer beef franks
1 can (8 oz.) baked beans
1 can (8 oz.) kidney beans
1 can (8 oz.) lima beans, drained
1 can (8 oz.) tomato sauce
1 envelope (1¾ oz.) chili seasoning mix

Cut beef franks into ½-inch pieces. Combine with remaining ingredients in saucepan. Heat about 10 minutes, stirring frequently.

Barbecue Ham Jerky

This keeps about a week without refrigeration.

12 serving

1 can (3 lb.) Oscar Mayer ham (oblong)
1 quart barbecue sauce

Slice ham into ⅛-inch slices. Cut each slice into 3 strips (measuring 1x3½ inches). Marinate in barbecue sauce 15 minutes. Place strips on rack in shallow pan. Bake in 200°F oven for 4½ to 5 hours, until strips are dry, hard and snap when folded. Blot strips with paper towel. Store in airtight container.
220 calories/serving

Backyard Olympics for Kids!

Light the torch, raise the flags and sound a fanfare. With a little advance planning, your yard could be the site of the next Kids' Olympics. Get out the stopwatch and tape measure; put up a chalkboard to list events and winners. Set up the races—on tricycles, in potato sacks and under hurdles.

Judge cartwheels, somersaults, hops, skips and jumps. Hold a softball throw and set up an obstacle course.

Have the awards ceremony on the top step of the front porch. Hang homemade medals (made with ribbon and foil-covered chocolate coins) around each proud winner's neck.

The Best in the West

*T*he "Spaghetti Western" was a nickname given to low-grade shoot-'em-up cowboy movies which were filmed in Italy to save money. But you can turn it into a rootin' tootin' party theme. Round up your friends, all dressed casually in boots and jeans, and put on the country-western tunes. Part of the fun will be naming your dishes. "Get-along-little-doggies" are cocktail size wieners in barbecue sauce. Form softened cheese into a cowboy hat shape and it's a "10-gallon" cheeseball. Stir up a wild cowpuncher's punch. Toss a "Tall in the Saddle Salad" and heat up "Buckin' Bronco Ham Buns." And of course, serve hearty, meaty spaghetti. Prepare it a day ahead so you can spend most of your time with your partners doing the do-si-do!

If you're outside, set up horseshoes, a lariat for roping, water pistols for sharpshooting and put on a rodeo. You can build a quick chuckwagon with a sheet, some wire and picnic tables. Indoors, you may want to show—what else—old western movies!

Vegetable Ham Kabobs

8 servings

1 can (1½ lb.) Oscar Mayer ham, cut into 16 cubes
2 medium green peppers, cut into 8 pieces
2 medium zucchini, cut into 8 chunks
2 ears corn, cut into fourths
1 cup barbecue sauce
8 metal skewers

Alternate ham and vegetables on skewers. Heat 3 to 4 inches from coals about 20 minutes, turning occasionally. Baste with barbecue sauce the last 10 minutes of heating.
165 calories/serving

Charcoal Grilled Ham

12 servings

1 can (3 lb.) Oscar Mayer ham
½ cup barbecue sauce

Cut ham in half to form 2 pieces, each 1½ to 2 inches thick. Heat 3 to 4 inches from coals 30 to 45 minutes, turning occasionally. Baste with barbecue sauce the last 15 minutes of heating.

Charcoal Grilled Franks in Beer

10 servings

½ cup butter
1 onion, thinly sliced and separated into rings
1 can (12 oz.) beer
1 package (16 oz.) Oscar Mayer beef franks
10 hot dog buns

Melt butter in saucepan. Add onion and cook until tender. Add beer. Heat franks 3 to 4 inches from coals 10 minutes, turning occasionally. Serve franks in buns; spoon sauce over franks.

Dough Boys

8 servings

1 package (12 oz.) Oscar Mayer "Smokie Links"
2 cups buttermilk baking mix
½ cup cold water

Pat Smokie Links dry with paper towel. Combine baking mix and water in bowl to form soft dough. Divide into 8 equal parts. Wrap dough around each link. Insert grilling stick into wrapped link or place on sheet of aluminum foil on grill. Heat 3 to 4 inches from coals 15 to 20 minutes until golden brown.

Get Into Camping Out

*C*amping is a time for fellowship and fun. When you're in charge of campfire activities, try a nature scavenger hunt. Write up a list of ordinary and rare items you

might be able to find (oak leaves, pine cones, fossils, fishhooks; try bottle caps—specify the brand to make it harder—or butterflies). You might even make up a fantasy item or two. Divide into teams and see who fills the list first.

Make a special campfire snack by wrapping Smokie Links with biscuit mix and roasting over the fire. Dipped in butter and cinnamon-sugar, it makes a great breakfast feast, too!

Summer Stir-Fry

4 servings

- 1 package (6 oz.) Oscar Mayer smoked cooked ham
- 2 tablespoons vegetable oil
- ¼ teaspoon garlic powder
- 1 package (16 oz.) frozen mixed vegetables
- 1 small onion, cut into wedges
- 1 package (6 oz.) frozen pea pods and water chestnuts
- 1 cup (2 oz.) sliced fresh mushrooms

Sauce:
- 1 bottle (8 oz.) Russian salad dressing
- 2 tablespoons soy sauce

Cut ham into ½-inch strips. Set aside. Heat oil in wok or skillet on medium-high 3 minutes; add garlic, mixed vegetables and onion. Stir-fry vegetables 5 minutes until tender-crisp. Add remaining ingredients continuing to stir-fry 3 to 5 minutes more. Combine sauce ingredients. Serve with stir-fry.

Sweet and Sour Kabobs

4 servings

- 1 package (16 oz.) Oscar Mayer jumbo wieners
- 1 pint cherry tomatoes
- 2 green peppers, cut into 1-inch pieces
- 1 can (8¼ oz.) pineapple chunks, drained
- ¾ cup sweet-sour sauce, bottled or prepared from a package
- 2 tablespoons soy sauce
- 8 metal skewers

Cut wieners into thirds. To make kabobs: alternate wiener pieces on skewers with tomatoes, green pepper and pineapple. Arrange in single layer on broiler pan. Combine sweet-sour sauce and soy sauce. Brush kabobs with sauce. Broil 4 inches from heat 4 minutes or until bubbling. Turn. Brush with sauce. Broil 5 minutes more.

Chow Mein Salad

4 serving

- 1 package (8 oz.) Oscar Mayer honey loaf
- 1 package (6 oz.) pea pods, thawed
- 1 can (8 oz.) sliced water chestnuts, drained
- 1 cup (2 oz.) sliced fresh mushrooms
- 2 cups shredded Chinese cabbage
- ½ cup chow mein noodles

Dressing:
- ½ cup plain yogurt
- ¼ cup mayonnaise
- 3 green onions, chopped
- 1 tablespoon soy sauce
- 8 drops bottled hot pepper sauce

Slice meat into ¼-inch strips. Toss with pea pods, water chestnuts and mushrooms. Arrange on cabbage-lined platter. Sprinkle with chow mein noodles. Combine dressing ingredients. Serve with salad.

A 5,000-Year-Old Celebration With a Bang

Since the Chinese invented paper and firecrackers, it's only appropriate that they parade huge paper dragons and shoot fireworks on Chinese New Year. Officially, it's the first new moon between January 21 and February 19. So if you have a yen, ring out the Yin (dark, evil) and ring in the Yang (light, good) right along with them.

Bring out the chopsticks and Chow Mein Salad, followed by Chinese Pepper Strips. Be sure to have lots of hot green tea and fortune cookies with hilarious messages. If someone you know can write Chinese characters have them print each guest's name on a place card. It makes a great Happy New Year souvenir.

Post "Confucius Says" teachings and this chart:

Each year has a personality. What's yours?

Their Year			Our Year			
Rat	1924	1936	1948	1960	1972	1984
Ox	1925	1937	1949	1961	1973	1985
Tiger	1926	1938	1950	1962	1974	1986
Hare	1927	1939	1951	1963	1975	1987
Dragon	1928	1940	1952	1964	1976	1988
Serpent	1929	1941	1953	1965	1977	1989
Horse	1930	1942	1954	1966	1978	1990
Ram	1931	1943	1955	1967	1979	1991
Monkey	1932	1944	1956	1968	1980	1992
Rooster	1933	1945	1957	1969	1981	1993
Dog	1934	1946	1958	1970	1982	1994
Boar	1935	1947	1959	1971	1983	1995

Honey Loaf Lettuce Rolls

4 servings

1 package (10 oz.) frozen Japanese-style vegetables in sauce, thawed
1 can (8 oz.) sliced water chestnuts, drained
8 large iceberg lettuce leaves
1 package (8 oz.) Oscar Mayer honey loaf
½ cup water
1 tablespoon dry sherry
½ teaspoon instant chicken bouillon
4 servings hot cooked rice

Combine vegetables and water chestnuts in large bowl. Trim rib of each lettuce leaf. Place 1 slice meat and ¼ cup vegetable mixture in center of each lettuce leaf. Fold sides of lettuce leaf toward center over meat. Roll up jelly-roll fashion. Place in large skillet, seam-side down. Add water, sherry and bouillon. Cover. Bring to a boil. Turn down heat. Simmer 10 minutes. Spoon rice onto serving platter. Arrange lettuce rolls on top. Cover and keep warm. Cook bouillon mixture on high 5 minutes to reduce liquid to ½ cup. Serve with lettuce rolls and rice. 315 calories/serving

Microwave: Combine sherry and bouillon (no water is needed) in 12x7-inch glass baking dish. Prepare lettuce rolls as above; add to baking dish. Microwave at HIGH 8 to 9 minutes, rotating dish after four minutes. Spoon rice onto serving platter. Arrange lettuce rolls on top. Heat sauce 30 to 90 seconds until hot and bubbly. Serve as above.

For a Party with a Nice Hawaiian Punch, Have a Luau

Imagine grass skirts swaying to the strum of a ukulele, the gentle scent of orchids in the air. You don't have to go to Hawaii to have all this. Hold a Hawaiian Luau in your own backyard. Greet your guests at the door with a flower lei (plastic or crepe paper ones may be easier to come by) and a kiss. Gentle Hawaiian music sets the mood, along with decorations like conch shells, orchids, travel posters, and flaming torches. The food will make the party, so be sure to have some fresh pineapples, chunks of coconut and maybe some poi as a novelty. Have Hawaiian dancers perform. Make sure they explain what some of the hand motions mean. And be sure to get everyone up doing the hula.

Hibachi Kabobs

8 appetizers

1 package (5 oz.) Oscar Mayer "Little Wieners"
1 package (5½ oz.) Oscar Mayer "Little Smokies"
1 can (8 oz.) pineapple chunks, with liquid
1 lemon, sliced
2 oranges, cut into wedges
8 (6-inch) metal skewers
Honey Sauce*

Thread skewers alternating Little Wieners, Little Smokies and fruit. Grill on hibachi. Brush with Honey Sauce; turn occasionally until heated through.

*Honey Sauce:
⅓ cup pineapple liquid (reserved from canned pineapple chunks)
¼ cup honey
1 tablespoon lemon juice
2 teaspoons cornstarch
½ teaspoon celery seed
¼ teaspoon paprika

Combine all ingredients in saucepan; heat to boiling, stirring constantly. Cook until thickened. 195 calories/serving

Ham Polynesian

2 servin

1 package (8 oz.) Oscar Mayer ham slice
2 tablespoons butter
1 can (8¼ oz.) pineapple chunk with liquid
1 green pepper, cut into strips
¼ cup brown sugar
1 tablespoon cornstarch
¼ cup vinegar
2 teaspoons soy sauce
1 teaspoon instant chicken bouillon
¼ cup water
2 servings hot cooked rice

Cut ham slice into ½-inch strips Melt butter in skillet on medium Heat ham until lightly browned; add pineapple and green pepper. Cover. Simmer 5 to 10 minutes until green pepper is tender-crisp Combine brown sugar, cornstarch vinegar, soy sauce, bouillon and water in bowl; blend well. Gradually add to ham mixture; cook 5 minutes more, stirring constantly until mixture thicken and boils. Serve over rice.

Chinese Pepper Strips

6 servings

1 package (16 oz.) Oscar Mayer beef franks
2 tablespoons vegetable oil
1 medium onion, sliced
1 can (4 oz.) mushroom stems and pieces, drained
1/8 teaspoon garlic powder
3 tablespoons soy sauce
2 tablespoons cornstarch
1 can (10½ oz.) beef broth
2 green peppers, cut into 1-inch squares
2 tomatoes, cut into eighths
6 servings hot cooked rice

ut each frank into 4 lengthwise
rips. Heat oil in skillet on
edium. Add franks, onion,
ushrooms and garlic. Cook 10
inutes stirring occasionally.
ombine soy sauce, cornstarch and
roth in bowl; blend well.
radually add to frank mixture;
ok, stirring constantly until
uce thickens and boils. Stir in
een pepper and tomato. Cover.
emove from heat; let stand
veral minutes until vegetables
heated through. Serve over
ce.

Bacon Fried Rice

4 servings

0 slices Oscar Mayer bacon
4 cups cooked rice
1 can (4 oz.) mushrooms, drained
2 green onions, chopped
2 eggs, slightly beaten
2 tablespoons soy sauce

t bacon into 1-inch pieces. Cook
skillet on medium-low until
sp. Remove bacon. Add rice,
ushrooms and onion to
ippings. Cook on medium,
rring quickly to coat rice. Stir in
gs, soy sauce and bacon. Cook 5
nutes, stirring frequently.

Oriental Soup

4 servings

2 eggs, beaten
2 tablespoons water
1 tablespoon butter
8 slices Oscar Mayer "Lean 'n Tasty" breakfast strips
4 cups water
4 teaspoons instant chicken bouillon
2 green onions, chopped

Combine eggs and 2 tablespoons
water in small bowl. Melt butter in
large skillet on medium-low. Add
egg mixture. Cook until set, lifting
edges to allow uncooked portion to
flow underneath. Cool. Cut egg
into 3x¼-inch strips; set aside.
Cut breakfast strips into 3x½-inch
strips. Combine with 4 cups water,
bouillon and onion in saucepan.
Bring to a boil. Turn down heat.
Simmer 5 minutes. Stir in egg
strips. Serve immediately.
290 calories/serving

Smokie Chop Suey

4 servings

1 package (12 oz.) Oscar Mayer "Smokie Links"
1 can (13¾ oz.) chicken broth
3 tablespoons cornstarch
3 tablespoons soy sauce
1 teaspoon sugar
2 stalks celery, sliced diagonally
1 can (8 oz.) sliced water chestnuts, drained
1 can (16 oz.) bean sprouts, drained
4 servings hot cooked rice

Cut Smokie Links diagonally into
chunks. Combine broth,
cornstarch, soy sauce and sugar in
large skillet. Bring to a boil,
stirring constantly until mixture
thickens. Turn down heat. Stir in
celery, water chestnuts, bean
sprouts and Smokie Links. Simmer
5 minutes. Serve over rice.

Bacon Egg Foo Yung

6 servings

10 slices Oscar Mayer bacon
6 eggs, beaten
3 tablespoons cornstarch
1 can (16 oz.) bean sprouts, drained
1 can (4 oz.) mushroom stems and pieces, drained
1 green onion, finely chopped
1/8 teaspoon pepper
Sauce:
1¼ cups water
1 teaspoon instant beef bouillon
1 tablespoon cornstarch
1 tablespoon soy sauce

Cut bacon into ½-inch pieces.
Cook in skillet on medium-low
until crisp. Remove bacon; reserve
drippings. Combine eggs and
cornstarch in bowl; blend well. Stir
in bacon, bean sprouts,
mushrooms, onion, and pepper.
Heat 1 teaspoon drippings on
medium in small skillet. Add ¼
cup bacon-egg mixture. Cook,
turning once, until both sides are
lightly browned. Remove from
skillet. Cover and keep warm.
Repeat with remaining bacon-egg
mixture adding more drippings to
skillet as needed. To make sauce:
heat 1 cup water to boiling. Add
bouillon; stir until dissolved.
Combine cornstarch, soy sauce and
remaining ¼ cup water; add to hot
bouillon. Cook until mixture
thickens and boils, stirring
constantly. Serve Egg Foo Yung
with sauce.
230 calories/serving

Why Not a Party From Japan?

Have everyone take off their
shoes at the door. Bring
out the hibachi, wok,
chopsticks. Sit on the floor.
Decorate with little bonsai trees
and celebrate setsubun, (bean
throwing festival) on February
3 or Children's Day on May 5.

Breakfast Burrito

1 serving

- 2 slices Oscar Mayer cotto salami
- 1 large flour tortilla, 7-inch diameter
- 1 tablespoon butter
- 1 egg, beaten
- 2 tablespoons shredded Cheddar cheese
- 1 tablespoon chopped onion Chili powder

Overlap meat on tortilla. Melt butter in small skillet. Add tortilla with meat. Top with egg, cheese and onion. Cover. Cook on medium-low heat 5 minutes or until egg is set. Sprinkle with chili powder; fold in half.

Microwave: Place butter in glass pie plate. Microwave at HIGH about 30 seconds. Spread butter to coat bottom; add egg. Sprinkle with cheese and onion. Cover with waxed paper. Microwave at HIGH 1 to 1½ minutes until set, rotating plate after thirty seconds. Sprinkle with chili powder; top with meat. Loosen edges; slide cooked egg and meat onto tortilla. Roll up or fold over.

Tortilla Stack

4 servings

- 1 package (8 oz.) Oscar Mayer cotto salami
- 1 cup (4 oz.) shredded Cheddar cheese
- 5 flour tortillas, 6-inch diameter
- 1 can (4 oz.) chopped green chilies, drained
- 1 small onion, finely chopped
- 1 tablespoon butter, melted
- ½ cup (4 oz.) taco sauce

Set aside 2 slices meat and 1 tablespoon cheese. Place a tortilla on shallow baking pan. Top with 2 slices meat, ¼ of chilies, onions and cheese. Repeat layers ending with tortilla. Brush with butter. Bake in 350°F oven 35 minutes. Top with reserved meat and cheese. Bake 5 minutes more. Let stand 5 minutes. Cut into fourths. Serve with taco sauce.
345 calories/serving

Microwave: Set aside 2 slices meat and 1 tablespoon cheese. Assemble as above except omit butter; place on plate. Microwave at HIGH 6 to 7 minutes, rotating plate a half turn after three minutes. Top with reserved meat and cheese. Microwave 1 minute more. Cover. Let stand 5 minutes. Serve as above.

Puerto Rican Chicken Breasts

2 servin

- 1 whole chicken breast, boned, skinned and cut in half
- ¼ teaspoon garlic powder
- ¼ teaspoon onion powder
- ¼ teaspoon oregano leaves Dash pepper
- 2 slices process American chee
- 4 slices Oscar Mayer bacon

Sauce:
- ¼ cup white wine
- 2 teaspoons vinegar
- 2 teaspoons olive oil

Place chicken between pieces of waxed paper. Pound to flatten with a rolling pin or mallet. Remove paper. Combine seasonings and sprinkle half over chicken. Place cheese slice on eac roll up. Sprinkle with remaining seasonings. Wrap each with 2 bacon slices. Place in small shall baking dish. Combine sauce ingredients; pour over chicken. Bake in 375°F oven 45 minutes o until golden brown.

Go a Little Loco With a Mexican Fiesta

It started as a children's game, but everybody loves a piñata. It's a colorful, festively decorated animal, star or figure made out of paper mache. The piñata is filled with candy, toys, coins and prizes. During the party the piñata serves as a decoration but it later becomes the grand finale. Guests are blindfolded one at a time and handed a long stick. As the piñata swings in the air, the blindfolded person tries to break it open with the stick. Everybody gets a turn until the piñata finally spills its surprises!

How to Make a Real Piñata

You can make your own piñatas with various shaped balloons, strips of old newspaper, and a paste of flour, salt and water. Build the shape you want with balloons: a burro, rooster, pig or unicorn; perhaps a sombrero or a free-form shape may be more to your liking. Cover the balloons with 2-inch wide strips of newspaper soaked in the flour paste. Let the first layer dry overnight or speed up the process with a hair dryer. Then add another layer of paper mache. Design a loop on top for hanging. When the last layer dries, pop the balloons inside with a pin. Carefully cut a hole in the side or top, fill the piñata with prizes and patch the opening. Then paint the paper mache with bright colors, adding crepe-paper streamers, glitter and other festive decorations for a colorful fiesta!

Music-Making Jamboree

You may not sound like a mariachi band, but when you get together and make your own instruments, you'll have some good sound fun. Make box drums and tom-toms. Put plastic wrap over a comb for a great kazoo. String up rubber bands to pluck, or build a wash tub bass with a string and stick. Lids from your pans make great castanets. Bottles with dried beans are great maracas. And glasses filled with different levels of water become a perfect marimba when rubbed on the rim or tapped with a spoon. For a windy tuba sound, blow into pop bottles filled with different amounts of water. You all can make beautiful music together.

Wiener Burritos

10 sandwiches

10 flour tortillas, 7-inch diameter
1 can (16 oz.) refried beans
½ cup (4 oz.) taco sauce
10 slices (¾ oz. each) process American cheese
1 package (16 oz.) Oscar Mayer wieners
¼ cup butter, melted

For each burrito, spread 2 tablespoons beans down center of tortilla. Top beans with 2 teaspoons taco sauce and 1 slice cheese. Place wiener at edge of tortilla; roll up. Place burritos, seam-side down on shallow baking pan. Brush each burrito with butter. Bake in 400°F oven 20 minutes until tortilla is golden.

Guacamole

3 cups

10 slices Oscar Mayer bacon
2 avocados, peeled and pitted
2 medium tomatoes
1 small onion
1 tablespoon lemon juice
¾ teaspoon bottled hot pepper sauce
¼ teaspoon garlic powder

Cut bacon into ½-inch pieces. Cook in skillet on medium-low until crisp; drain. Coarsely chop avocado and tomato in food processor using knife blade. Transfer to bowl. Finely chop onion using knife blade. Combine all ingredients. Chill 1 hour.

Bueno Potato Skins

4 servings

5 slices Oscar Mayer bacon
2 large baking potatoes
1 tablespoon butter, melted
1 tablespoon green chilies, chopped
2 tablespoons chopped tomato
½ cup (2 oz.) shredded Cheddar cheese
Chili powder
Sour cream

Cut bacon into ½-inch pieces. Bake potatoes in 400°F oven 1 hour or until fork tender. Meanwhile cook bacon in skillet on medium-low until crisp; drain. Cut cooked potatoes in half lengthwise; scoop out leaving ¼-inch shell. Use scooped out potatoes at another meal. Brush shell with butter. Broil 5 inches from heat 3 minutes or until lightly browned around edges. Sprinkle with bacon pieces, chilies, tomatoes and cheese. Broil 1 to 2 minutes more until cheese melts. Sprinkle with chili powder. Serve with sour cream.

Bologna Rellenos

12 serving

2 packages (12 oz. each) Oscar Mayer bologna
1 package (16 oz.) flour tortillas 8-inch diameter
1 package (8 oz.) Monterey Jack cheese, cut into 12 (½-inch) strips
12 mild banana peppers
½ cup (4 oz.) taco sauce
Oil for frying or ¼ cup melted butter for baking
Toothpicks

Frying Method: For each serving, place 2 slices meat on a tortilla. Top with 1 strip cheese and 1 pepper; roll up and secure with toothpicks. Heat oil (about inch deep) in heavy skillet or de fat fryer to 350°F. Fry in hot oil to 3 minutes, turning to brown evenly on all sides. Drain on pap toweling. Heat taco sauce. Serve over Bologna Rellenos.

Baking Method: For each serving, place 2 slices bologna or each tortilla. Top with 1 strip cheese and 1 pepper; fold oppos edges over filling and tuck ends under. Place meat packets seam side down on ungreased baking sheet; brush generously with butter. Bake in 400°F oven 15 t 20 minutes until crisp and golde brown. Heat taco sauce. Serve o Bologna Rellenos.

Little Smokies wit Taco Cheese Sauc

32-64 appetize

1 container (8 oz.) sharp Cheddar cold pack cheese fo
½ cup (4 oz.) taco sauce
2 to 4 packages (5 oz. each) Osca Mayer "Little Smokies"

Combine cheese and taco sauce i saucepan. Cook on medium 5 minutes or until melted, stirring constantly. Add Little Smokies. Heat 5 minutes more, stirring frequently. Serve with picks.

Arroz Mexicano

6 servings

⅓ cup olive oil
1 clove garlic, finely chopped
½ cups parboiled rice, uncooked
3 cups water
½ teaspoon salt
1 package (6 oz.) Oscar Mayer cooked ham
6 eggs
1 can (8 oz.) tomato sauce
Parsley

Heat ¼ cup olive oil and garlic in large paella pan or skillet. Stir in rice, water and salt. Bring to a boil. Turn down heat. Simmer 20 minutes until rice is tender and water is absorbed (do not stir). Heat ham in another skillet with remaining olive oil. Remove ham and arrange on cooked rice in paella pan. Fry eggs; place on ham. Heat tomato sauce in small saucepan. Spoon over eggs and rice. Garnish with parsley.

Wieners Olé

4 servings

1 package (16 oz.) Oscar Mayer wieners
1 can (16 oz.) baked beans
1 can (8 oz.) tomato sauce
½ teaspoon chili powder
Few drops hot pepper sauce
½ cup (4 oz.) sour cream
¼ cup crushed corn chips

Cut wieners into penny slices. Combine with beans, tomato sauce, chili powder and hot pepper sauce in skillet. Bring to a boil. Turn down heat. Simmer 10 minutes. Top each serving with sour cream and corn chips.

Wiener Enchiladas

5 servings

2 cans (15 oz. each) mild enchilada sauce
10 flour tortillas, 7-inch diameter
1 package (16 oz.) Oscar Mayer wieners
1 medium onion, finely chopped
½ cup (4 oz.) shredded Cheddar cheese

Pour 1 can enchilada sauce in 13x9-inch pan. Roll a tortilla around each wiener. Place seam-side down in pan. Sprinkle with onion. Top with remaining can enchilada sauce. Bake in 350°F oven 30 minutes. Sprinkle with cheese.

Mexican Melt

1 serving

2 Oscar Mayer "Smokie Links"
½ package (12 oz.) frozen hashbrown potatoes
2 tablespoons vegetable oil
1 large slice onion, separated into rings
2 tablespoons chopped green chilies
1 slice process American cheese
Taco sauce

Cut Smokie Links lengthwise. Cook hashbrowns in oil 5 to 7 minutes; turn. Add Smokies and onion. Cook 2 to 3 minutes until lightly browned. Top hashbrowns with Smokies, onions, chilies and cheese. Cover. Heat 1 to 2 minutes until cheese melts.

Sausage Mexicali

4 servings

1 package (12 oz.) Oscar Mayer "Little Friers" pork sausage links
1 medium green pepper, chopped
1 medium onion, chopped
1 cup (4 oz.) uncooked elbow macaroni
1 can (16 oz.) tomatoes, undrained and cut into pieces
1 can (8 oz.) tomato sauce
1 teaspoon chili powder
½ cup sour cream

Cook sausage, green pepper and onion on medium 10 to 15 minutes until sausage is golden brown; drain. Add macaroni, tomatoes, tomato sauce and chili powder. Bring to a boil. Turn down heat. Cover. Simmer 15 minutes or until macaroni is tender. Garnish each serving with a dollop of sour cream.

Sonora Salad

4 servings

1 package (6 oz.) Oscar Mayer smoked cooked ham
2 cups cooked rice, chilled
3 medium (1 lb.) tomatoes, coarsely chopped
2 medium (8 oz.) green peppers, coarsely chopped
1 can (8 oz.) kidney beans, drained
Tortilla chips, if desired

Dressing:
1 bottle (8 oz.) taco sauce
¼ cup mayonnaise

Cut ham into thin strips. Toss meat, rice, tomatoes, peppers and beans in large bowl. Combine taco sauce and mayonnaise; blend into meat mixture. Chill thoroughly. Garnish with tortilla chips.

345 calories/serving

Choucroute Garni

8 servings

4 slices Oscar Mayer bacon
2 jars (32 oz. each) sauerkraut, drained
4 medium carrots, thinly sliced
3 medium onions, chopped
1 can (10¾ oz.) chicken broth
¾ cup dry white wine
12 whole black peppercorns
10 juniper berries, optional
1 package (16 oz.) Oscar Mayer wieners
1 package (12 oz.) Oscar Mayer ring bologna
1 package (8 oz.) Oscar Mayer ham steaks
1 package (5 oz.) Oscar Mayer "Little Smokies"

Cut bacon into 1-inch pieces. Cook in Dutch oven or large saucepot on medium-low until crisp. Add remaining ingredients except meat. Bring to a boil. Turn down heat. Cover. Simmer 15 minutes. Add meat. Cover. Simmer 15 minutes more.

Paula's German Pancake

2 servings

6 slices Oscar Mayer bacon
¼ cup butter
½ cup flour
½ cup milk
½ teaspoon salt
4 eggs
2 lemon wedges
  Confectioner's sugar
  Pancake syrup

Arrange bacon on rack in shallow pan; set aside until pancake is ready to bake. Melt butter in 10-inch ovenproof skillet. Combine flour, milk, salt and eggs in bowl; blend well. Pour egg mixture into skillet. Cook on medium until sides begin to set (center is still custard-like). Then place in oven. Bake pancake and bacon in 400°F oven 15 minutes until pancake is puffed and golden brown and bacon is crisp. Serve with lemon, confectioner's sugar and syrup.

Rotkohl

6 servings

10 slices Oscar Mayer bacon
2 medium apples, sliced into thin wedges
2 medium onions, chopped
1 medium head red cabbage, shredded
½ cup red wine vinegar
2 tablespoons sugar
½ cup water
1 bay leaf
2 teaspoons salt
⅛ teaspoon ground cloves
3 tablespoons red wine, optional
3 tablespoons currant jelly

Cut bacon into 1-inch pieces. Cook bacon in Dutch oven on medium-low until crisp. Add apple wedges and onion. Cook on medium in drippings until apples are slightly browned and onion is transparent. Stir in cabbage, vinegar, sugar, water, bay leaf, salt and cloves. Cook on low 40 minutes, stirring occasionally. Stir in wine and jelly just before serving.

Hot German Potato Salad

4 to 6 servings

10 slices Oscar Mayer bacon
½ cup chopped celery
½ cup chopped onion
2 tablespoons flour
⅛ teaspoon black pepper
¼ cup water
½ cup cider vinegar
½ cup sugar
5 medium potatoes, cooked and sliced

Cut bacon into 1-inch pieces. Cook in large skillet on medium-low until crisp; remove bacon. Add celery and onion to skillet; cook until tender. Blend in flour; stir in water, vinegar and sugar. Cook on medium stirring until thickened. Add bacon and potatoes; stir. Cover. Heat 5 minutes.

Roll out the Barrel and Celebrate Oktoberfest!

Oktoberfest in Germany means weeks of beer, brats and celebration. Put up a tent, tap a keg and you've got a backyard celebration of your own!

Decorate with colorful beer steins, put up a cuckoo clock and hang streamers all around. Hire a polka band, show your guests the basic step and have a rousin' good time. Men should wear lederhosen (suspendered shorts which show off their knees). Ladies can lace up in dirndles.

Serve Choucroute Garni— sausages and sauerkraut—along with Black Forest cake or

strudel for dessert. And make sure to have plenty of brew on hand for all those thirsty dancers!

Beef Rouladen

6 servings

6 slices Oscar Mayer bacon
2½ to 3 pounds round steak, cut ¼-inch thick
¼ cup Dijon mustard
1 large onion, chopped
3 kosher dill pickles, cut lengthwise into quarters
2 tablespoons oil
1 cup water
1 teaspoon instant chicken bouillon
1 can (8 oz.) tomato sauce
1 bay leaf
12 ounces medium noodles
  Toothpicks
2 tablespoons flour
¼ cup water

Cut bacon slices in half. Trim steak removing bone and excess fat. Divide into 12 pieces. Pound into approximately 8x4-inch pieces. Top each piece with 1 teaspoon mustard, 1 tablespoon onion and ½ bacon slice. Lay pickle across narrow end of each piece. Roll up; secure with toothpicks. Brown meat in oil in large skillet. Add water, bouillon, tomato sauce and bay leaf. Cover. Bring to a boil. Turn down heat. Simmer 1 to 1½ hours until tender. Cook noodles according to package directions; drain. Place on platter. Remove toothpicks from meat rolls; place on noodles. Cover to keep warm. Mix flour and water. Stir into sauce in skillet. Cook on medium, stirring constantly until mixture thickens and boils. Serve with beef rolls and noodles.

Old World Sausage Soup

6 servings

1 package (12 oz.) Oscar Mayer "Smokie Links"
2 carrots, thinly sliced
1 small head cabbage, shredded (about 1½ pounds)
1 quart water
1 can (16 oz.) white beans, undrained
1 can (16 oz.) kidney beans, undrained
2 teaspoons instant chicken bouillon
½ teaspoon thyme
¼ teaspoon pepper

Cut Smokie Links into ½-inch pieces. Combine all ingredients in Dutch oven. Bring to a boil; reduce heat. Simmer 20 minutes until vegetables are tender.

Tyrolean Green Beans

6 serving

10 slices Oscar Mayer bacon
1 small onion, chopped
2 pounds fresh green beans
1 teaspoon sugar
1 tablespoon vinegar

Cut bacon in ½-inch pieces. Cook bacon and onion in skillet on medium-low until bacon is crisp and onion tender; drain. Cook green beans; drain. Stir in bacon, onion, sugar and vinegar. Heat on medium 5 minutes, stirring occasionally.

"Silhouettes on the Shade"

Old world farmers used to watch the badger as a guide for planting. If he came out on February 2 and saw his shadow, they knew there would be six more weeks of winter. But the Germans who came to the New World couldn't find a badger—so, they used the groundhog instead.

Although the groundhog is seldom right about the weather, he does provide a great excuse for what else—a shadow party. Set up a sheet with a light behind it. Put on skits, charades and shadow dances. Make animal shadows with your hands. Have everyone dress in black or white. Play tapes of old Shadow (. . . only The Shadow knows) radio programs. And don't forget nostalgic tunes like "The Shadow of Your Smile" and "Me and My Shadow."

Brotzeit

4 servings

1 package (12 oz.) Oscar Mayer "Little Friers" pork sausage
1 onion, sliced and separated into rings
1 can (12 oz.) beer
4 hard rolls

ook sausage in skillet according package directions. Reserve 2 ablespoons drippings in skillet. dd onion; cook on medium until nder. Add beer. Cover. Bring to boil. Turn down heat. Simmer 15 inutes. Place 3 sausage links in ach roll. Spoon onion sauce over nks.

Heidelberg Sausage Salad

4 servings

1 package (8 oz.) Oscar Mayer summer sausage
1 package (16 oz.) frozen broccoli, cauliflower and carrots
1 small cucumber, thinly sliced
1 small onion, thinly sliced and separated into rings
Lettuce leaves

ressing:
½ cup vegetable oil
¼ cup vinegar
½ teaspoon dry mustard
¼ teaspoon salt
⅛ teaspoon pepper

ut meat into ¼-inch strips. Cook getables until tender-crisp; ain. Toss with meat, cucumber d onion. Combine dressing gredients. Pour over meat ixture; mix well. Cover. Chill veral hours. Serve on lettuce aves.

Hot German Ham Sandwich

1 serving

2 slices Oscar Mayer smoked cooked ham
1 slice process Swiss cheese, cut diagonally
1 slice dark rye bread, toasted
2 tablespoons sauerkraut
1 teaspoon Italian salad dressing
1 teaspoon chopped green onion
3 kosher-style dill pickle slices

Fold ham around cheese triangles. Place on bread. Combine drained sauerkraut, dressing and onion. Spoon over ham; top with pickles. Place on shallow baking pan. Bake in 350°F oven 15 minutes or until cheese melts.
225 calories/serving

Microwave: Place assembled sandwich on paper towel on paper plate. Microwave at HIGH 1 minute or until cheese melts.

Rhine Stew

8 servings

2 packages (12 oz. each) Oscar Mayer "Little Friers" pork sausage links
1 can (16 oz.) kidney beans
1 can (16 oz.) white beans
1 can (16 oz.) sliced carrots
1 can (16 oz.) stewed tomatoes
⅛ teaspoon garlic powder
1 tablespoon dried parsley flakes

Cook pork sausage; drain. Pour liquid off kidney beans, white beans and carrots (for thinner consistency, do not drain). Combine sausage, vegetables and seasonings in Dutch oven. Bring to a boil. Reduce heat. Simmer 15 minutes.

Throw a Talent Show

The invitations can look like movie-production clap boards, or be written on pairs of novelty sunglasses. You're going to host a "talent show." To get in, everybody must have a skit, song or other entertaining specialty. Rent a videotape camera for the event, and capture it all on film. It'll provide lots of laughs when you replay it. You'll need a main stage, some sort of seating and big signs that read "APPLAUSE," "LAUGH" and "GROAN." Set up a panel of judges and award prizes afterwards. For fun, you can have some quick-drying plaster of Paris mixed up and have all your "stars" put a handprint and signature in wet plaster, just like in Hollywood.

Bavarian Kraut

6 servings

10 slices Oscar Mayer bacon
2 medium onions, chopped
1 pound fresh mushrooms, sliced
1 jar (32 oz.) sauerkraut, drained

Cut bacon into 1-inch pieces. Cook bacon and onion in large skillet on medium-low until bacon is crisp and onion is tender. Add mushrooms; cook about 5 minutes. Add sauerkraut. Stir occasionally until heated through. Serve with bratwurst, Smokie Links sausage or ¼ pound beef franks.

Party Meat Platter

An attractive party platter adds a festive touch to any occasion. It's easy and it's fun . . . just keep these six tips in mind:

- Vary the shape, color and texture of the meats.

  Choose round sausage like bologna, New England, and salami for beer and square meats like honey loaf, luncheon meat and luxury loaf.

  Choose light colored meats like smoked cooked ham, turkey and beef bologna and dark meats like cotto salami, roast beef, summer sausage.

  Choose smooth textures like liver cheese and honey loaf or mosaic meats like olive loaf, head cheese and ham and cheese loaf.

- Add dimension and interest by folding, rolling and wrapping the meats; cut into squares or wedges.

- Line the platter with lettuce. Select a tray large enough to accommodate four slices of meat or cheese per person.

- Garnish the tray with fresh fruit or vegetables, creating a focal point in the center.

- Cover with plastic wrap and refrigerate several hours or overnight.

- Serve with spreads like mayonnaise, or this Creamy Mustard Dunk:

Creamy Mustard Dunk:
Combine 1 cup (8 oz.) sour cream, 2 tablespoons mustard, 2 teaspoons instant minced onion and ¼ teaspoon horseradish. Cover and chill 1 hour.

Index